LEARNING THROUGH FIELD INSTRUCTION

A Guide for Teachers and Students

MARTHA L. URBANOWSKI
MARGARET M. DWYER

Family Service America
Milwaukee, Wisconsin

Copyright © 1988
Family Service America
11700 West Lake Pake Drive
Milwaukee, Wisconsin 53224

All rights reserved. None of the content of this publication may be reproduced, stored in a retrieval system, or transmitted in any form or by any means (electronic, mechanical, photocopying, recording, or otherwise) without the prior written permission of the publisher.

Library of Congress Cataloging-in-Publication Data

Urbanowski, Martha L.
  Learning through field instruction : a guide for teachers and students / Martha L. Urbanowski, Margaret M. Dwyer.
    p. cm.
  Bibliography: p.
  ISBN 0-87304-220-4
  1. Social work education — United States. 2. Social service — United States — Field work. 3. Social service — Field work — Study and teaching — United States. I. Dwyer, Margaret M. II. Title.
  HV11.U73 1988
  361.3'2'071173 — dc19   88-16494
                                                                          CIP

Printed in the United States

This book is dedicated to field instructors and students of Loyola University of Chicago School of Social Work and the Social Work Department of the College of Arts and Sciences.

CONTENTS

	Foreword	vii
	Preface	ix
1.	RESPONSIBILITIES FOR FIELD INSTRUCTION: IDENTIFICATION AND IMPLEMENTATION	1
2.	GUIDELINES FOR UNDERSTANDING THE PHASES OF LEARNING	17
3.	INDIVIDUALIZING THE LEARNER	29
4.	RECORDING	43
5.	PROCESS RECORDING	53
6.	LEARNING PATTERNS IN FIELD PRACTICE	61
7.	STUDENT VIEWS OF THE FIELD INSTRUCTOR	75
8.	VALUE OF FIELD-PRACTICE CRITERIA TO MEASURE PERFORMANCE	85
9.	SUGGESTED CRITERIA FOR UNDERGRADUATE FIELD-PRACTICE PERFORMANCE	91
10.	SUGGESTED CRITERIA FOR GRADUATE FIELD-PRACTICE PERFORMANCE	107
11.	THE ROLE AND USE OF THE FACULTY LIAISON	121
	ANNOTATED BIBLIOGRAPHY	133
	APPENDIX A: SAMPLE PROCESS RECORDING	149
	APPENDIX B: SAMPLE RECORDING TO PREPARE FOR PROFESSIONAL PRACTICE	159
	APPENDIX C: ROLE PLAY	163
	APPENDIX D: UNDERGRADUATE FIELD-PRACTICE EVALUATION FORM	169

FOREWORD

ONE OF THE MOST IMPORTANT areas of concern in social services today is the professional training of social workers. The Council on Social Work Education, the national accrediting agency for social work education, emphasizes the importance of field instruction as an integral component of social work education. Accordingly, schools of social work entrust part of their students' education to various agencies and their staffs who provide practicum settings for social work students. Therefore, it is appropriate that someone with agency administration and practice experience introduce this text.

Martha Urbanowski and Margaret Dwyer are to be commended for writing a book that presents a practical approach to managing important components of field instruction. Their book provides linkages among schools of social work and their faculty liaisons, agencies and their field instructors, and students.

Countless articles and books have been written on the subjects of field instruction and supervision. However, to my knowledge, this book is the first to deal succinctly with the many practical details associated with educating students in various agency and program settings.

Learning through Field Instruction should be particularly useful in providing guidance for understanding the different learning phases and styles of the students as well as the goals and objectives associated with process recording. The text provides examples of student contracts and evaluation forms, and it describes role expectations for faculty liaisons and field instructors.

Students, field instructors, and faculty liaisons will appreciate the fact that the material in the book is immediately applicable. Field instructors may use the book to increase their skills and understanding through self-study or advanced training. Students, on the other hand, may gain a more realistic view of field instructors after reading the text as well as a broader understanding of social work education.

The authors have defined and articulated criteria for both undergraduate and graduate field-practice performance. These criteria will be valuable to agencies that are involved in the training of both undergraduate and graduate students. They provide a baseline from which the schools and agencies can develop a dialogue.

In summary, *Learning through Field Instruction* is well-conceived and well-presented. It is an excellent attempt at coordinating the efforts of schools of social work and agencies in the mission of training professional social workers. It should be in the library of every agency that provides practicum settings as well as every school of social work. Furthermore, it should be required reading for persons who are responsible for field education.

CARL P. DOEING
Director, Substance Abuse Program
State of New Mexico

PREFACE

ALTHOUGH THE LITERATURE has expanded on the field-practice component of social work education, a need continues for more specific content and uniform guidelines for field instruction to improve teaching skills of the field instructor and promote learning in the student. Our purpose is to discuss field-instruction topics that we have found helpful for teaching colleagues who undertake field instruction and students who are learning in a practice setting.

Field instructors invest considerable time and effort in teaching students and require direction if they are to perform their role. The profession expects them to be competent practitioners, experts knowledgeable about the changing social work practice scene, role models, career counselors, and skilled teachers. The educational institutions, field-practice settings, and students place heavy demands on field instructors who assume these many roles. Frequently, field instructors are expected to shift roles from a practitioner to teacher with little formal preparation. They may rely heavily on their past experience in field practice or supervision and learn by trial and error. However, field instruction requires a planned academic focus, involved agencies, and committed field instructors to facilitate this role change or shift.

Students also invest considerable time and effort in their field-instruction courses. As in other academic courses, they need guidelines, ideas, and suggestions from the literature that will both stimulate and reassure them in their learning. Students demand quality education, especially in field-instruction courses. They are willing to invest in their learning but frequently are confused because expectations are vague or because they do not know how to achieve these expectations. Traditionally, training has focused on helping field instructors teach, with less emphasis on helping students learn in field instruction. However, students should be aware of current knowledge in field instruction.

This book provides some guidelines, suggestions, structure, and directions for both teaching and learning in field instruction. The responsibilities of all parties who are involved in the field instruction component of social work education are identified, and suggestions for carrying out these responsibilities are provided. The beginning, middle, and ending phases of learning are discussed. Understanding the phases of learning is basic to providing individualized instruction for the learner. This understanding is enhanced through the appropriate selection of learning experiences whereby students begin to integrate theoretical knowledge in the practice setting and become aware of their own feelings, attitudes, and responses toward the helping process. Identifying student learning patterns is essential for instructors to assist students to achieve their full potential. Although each student learns in his or her own way, some learning patterns are common to all students in field practice. General learning patterns are defined, behavioral characteristics of each are described, and some teaching approaches are suggested.

Discussions alone are not sufficient for understanding student learning needs or for determining the most effective teaching approach. Recording in its various forms—written, audio, and video—is a valuable teaching and learning tool; thus a structured framework for teaching through recording is included. Practice criteria to measure performance are suggested for both the undergraduate and graduate levels of performance. These criteria can be adjusted in accordance with the goals of the individual school and the expectations of the field-practice component of that school.

The school liaison to the practice setting plays a vital role in coordinating the agency, school, and student–field instructor relationship and ensures that the educational needs of each student are met. However, this function is often neglected. The responsibilities of the liaison are addressed and ways in which this role can be utilized for the benefit of all are discussed. The annotated bibliography includes selected articles, books, and monographs on field instruction. It should serve as a useful resource for classroom and field-instruction faculty, students, and others who are involved in the education of social work students.

We have spent the major part of our teaching careers in graduate and undergraduate field instruction. We feel a strong commitment to the process of teaching and learning in this sector of social work education and believe that a framework for the practice courses is essential. We are grateful to Felix P. Biestek, S.J., for his strong leadership and guidance throughout our careers as field instructors. He encouraged us to share our "practice wisdom" and volunteered his time to review the manuscript and suggest improvements. Fr. Biestek was an excellent role model for our professional growth and development. It is our hope that we can pass on to others the value and importance of the field-instruction component of social work education that he instilled in us. We are grateful also to the late Matthew H. Schoenbaum and Dean Charles T. O'Reilly of Loyola University of Chicago for promoting excellence in all components of social work education and never losing sight of the unique contribution of field practice.

MARTHA L. URBANOWSKI
Professor, Loyola University of Chicago

MARGARET M. DWYER
Professor, Loyola University of Chicago

1

RESPONSIBILITIES FOR FIELD INSTRUCTION: IDENTIFICATION AND IMPLEMENTATION

> *Field instruction is inevitably scrutinized because it is in field instruction that the student learns what to do and, in the main, learns what he should be. Field instruction is the mirror in which the profession sees not its image but its problems and in which professional education sees not its accomplishments but its failures. Class and field look into the mirror and ask, "who is the fairest of all?"*
>
> — Bernece K. Simon

Field-practice experience is a vital component in the education of social workers at the baccalaureate and master's degree levels. It occupies a large proportion of students' time relative to class curriculum and requires students to change and expand their ways of thinking, feeling, and doing. Field practice is crucial in determining a student's readiness for various levels of practice and in identifying the strengths and limitations of new practitioners. The Council on Social Work Education sets the standards and guidelines, and schools implement these requirements. However, success of the field-practice component of social work education requires the commitment of both educational institutions and the entire professional community. Without the contributions of staff of social service agencies who are involved in the teaching/learning process, field practice would be impossible and student learning would be drastically changed.

The social work profession is committed to field practice — both the educational institution and professional community want to continue to provide direct practice experience for social work students — and is expert in implementing this facet of the curriculum. Nonetheless, the gap between education and practice remains an area of concern, and bridging this gap is no easy assignment; the sharing of educational responsibility between agencies and schools will never be a placid and uneventful partnership. However, the partnership is worth maintaining despite the discomfort.[1]

Various models have been proposed and tested in order to strengthen the link between practice and education. Four models deserve brief mention.

1. *Training-Center Model:* This model calls for a mutually established center to meet the needs of both the educational institution and the agency and to help both expand their goals and quality of service.[2]

2. *Teaching-Center Model:* Utilized for a brief period during the 1960s and 1970s, this model attempts to organize field practice as an extension of the classroom. The students are assigned to a teaching center from which they may be sent to various agencies. Teaching experiences are determined by a sequence of educational principles rather than by assignments based on the needs of service settings.[3]

3. *Faculty-Based Field-Instruction-Unit Model:* Field instructors hired by the educational institution are placed in selected social agencies. They are conversant with school curriculum and attuned to the realities of agency practice. Many students can be accommodated in these units, and integration of theory with practice skills may be fostered at an accelerated pace.[4]

4. *Agency-Based Field-Instruction Model:* This more traditional model requires that selected social service agencies release sufficient time for qualified agency staff to work with students and schools of social work. Schools establish the conditions necessary for effective teaching and learning. Agencies provide space, equipment, teaching personnel, and learning opportunities that enable students to integrate theory with direct practice.[5]

Shrinking financial resources, time factors, educational values, and other professional considerations caused the early demise of the training-center and teaching-center models. A criticism of the teaching-center model was that it did not allow students to become sufficiently socialized into the profession.

The faculty-based field-instruction model is considered educationally sound and practice effective. It has many educational advantages in that field instructors are appointed by the faculty and share the responsibility of curriculum planning with the faculty. Unfortunately, changing funding patterns in the 1970s drastically reduced the number of faculty-based field-practice programs for the foreseeable future. Consequently, the social work profession has once again had to rely on the traditional agency-based field-instruction model.

The debate over issues of education and practice continues, regardless of the model that is used. In the 1960s schools were asked to recognize the importance of working with the top management of agencies on more than a superficial basis;[6] this issue remains a major concern in the 1980s. Harriet Bartlett responded to the age-old question of what blocks the lines of communication between education and practice.

> In order to teach, the educator must focus on the student, not on the client, and must transform the raw material of practice into concepts and principles. This focus and the process of abstraction remove the educator one step from the vital realities of practice. Furthermore, the terminology used in curriculum construction is not familiar to practitioners, so educators and practitioners are to a certain extent talking a different language. It is not surprising that they fail to communicate with one other.[7]

Field-instruction programs, however, are part of the partnership most frequently identified as needing attention.[8]

Literature that addresses the broad and specific issues of the field-practice component of social work education continues to be sparse, although some guidelines exist for agencies, field instructors, and students that help to identify responsibilities and translate tasks effectively. Margaret Schutz and William Gordon suggest a reallocation of educational responsibility whereby each institutional sector of the educational process would do what it is equipped to do.[9] Schools would produce certified graduates for training in practice, agencies would certify that students have demonstrated enough competence in practice to pass their licensing boards, the National Association of Social Workers (NASW) would certify agencies as qualified to take students for internship, and the Council on Social Work Education (CSWE) would strive to increase the quality and effectiveness of education through accreditation standards and procedures. Katherine Kendall emphasizes that social work education is a responsibility of the entire profession.[10] She describes the responsibilities of the school, agency, and professional organization, and also suggests that the general public, including board members, legislators, and interested citizens, has a stake in social work education. Francis Manis outlines the contributions and responsibilities of the field-instruction unit of the educational program, the student–agency administration, and the field instructor.[11] Suanna Wilson identifies the roles of key persons in the field-instruction process; key individuals include the agency, field instructor, school, faculty liaison, and student.[12] Bradford Sheafor and Lowell Jenkins devote an entire section of their book to the roles and responsibilities of the school, field-instruction agency, field instructor, and students.[13] They also include the rights and responsibilities of the clientele. Max Siporin identifies ten generic teaching principles that are applicable to all field-instruction settings.[14] Jean Granger and Signe Starnes describe roles within the administrative, educative, and supportive components of education as well as the interdependence and relationships among them.[15]

The present chapter focuses on two major areas of concern: (1) the responsibilities of the field-instruction setting, field instructor, educational institution, and student in the educational process, and (2) ways to implement these responsibilities.

FIELD INSTRUCTION SETTING

The achievement of educational harmony between the agency and academic institution requires that both be actively involved in the initial and ongoing educational plans for the social worker. Schools should examine and become familiar with various aspects of the agency before negotiating a placement arrangement or contract that is beneficial to both. Some of the constraints within agencies that might facilitate field instruction or present obstacles to it include the agency history, size, stage of development, specialization, financial support, nature of the task required, and agency role in the professional program.[16]

Many agency administrators feel that their programs are not given a fair appraisal and that they are excluded from much of the educational collaboration. In fact, agencies play a vital role in the education of social work students. Through the agency experience, students learn to function within an organizational structure that deals with people who are experiencing problems. Students must assume a new role and use their personal resources in a creative yet disciplined way while assuming responsibility for their own learning. In accepting an agency placement, students make an implicit, if not written, contract with an agency that includes (1) learning about the agency, (2) becoming familiar with services and rendering them to the best of their abilities, and (3) using appropriate agency and community resource systems. Schools must help agencies and students become knowledgeable about the various aspects of these contractual agreements. To expedite their part of the contract, agencies are responsible for (1) creating an atmosphere for learning, (2) providing a framework for learning organizational structure, (3) presenting an arena for professional development, and (4) offering educational supports.

Atmosphere for Learning

A major difficulty in helping students develop professional skills during field practice in social service agencies is described by Malcolm Knowles, a noted authority on adult learners:

> By and large, the adults we work with have not learned to be self-directing inquirers; they have been conditioned to be dependent on teachers to teach them. And so, they often experience a form of culture-shock when first exposed to truly educational programs.[17]

When people are faced with new and perhaps threatening situations, they tend to protect themselves, often feeling that they cannot contribute until they "know" and that they are unable to identify what they do know. Therefore, it is important that agencies create an atmosphere for adult learning that allows students to identify with the values and objectives of the profession. The professional climate for learning, with its prevailing values, attitudes, and taboos, plays a part in determining what pattern of response will dominate a practitioner's stance in regard to learning.[18]

Social agencies use a variety of approaches in dealing with human need, and service-delivery systems differ in purpose, function, and administrative structure. Many agencies are complex, rapidly changing organizations; students have much to learn before they are able to integrate agency practice expectations with the intellectual and behavioral objectives of the school.

Framework for Learning Organizational Structure

Students require help if they are to use the agency creatively in the interest of clients and in conjunction with other service units in the community. Each agency must be prepared to contribute to students' learning by providing a framework for understanding its organizational structure and patterns of operation through an ongoing orientation program. Throughout the orientation process, the agency staff should convey support and an attitude of interest, concern, and welcome. Students need to feel that they are a part of the agency, that they have the freedom to explore and question aspects of its operation. Agencies should afford the appropriate direction and steps for students to achieve these goals.

Arena for Professional Development

Agencies are the central arena for the development of professional identity. How professionals function within that setting sets an example of professional behavior that students eventually will emulate. Beginning social work students are extremely idealistic and frequently disappointed and sometimes shattered by what they observe in their placements. Part of the agency's task is to help students deal with the stark realities of the profession. More important, students need to know that the professional community is concerned and to understand the steps that are taken to remedy client situations. Students must be involved in changes within both the agency and the community, but they cannot be involved without direction and support. They must feel that their ideas are respected and that they have the freedom to express them. Although their thinking may be idealistic or come from a theoretical stance, this is the place where most begin.

In the field-practice setting, students observe and often identify with practitioners' attitudes toward professional organizations. The importance of participating in these organizations is learned more quickly by students in their practice experience than it is in discussions or lectures presented in classroom or professional organizations. Providing opportunities for students to participate in such organizations, indeed, is an essential responsibility of agencies toward the professional development of the social worker.

Educational Supports

The partnership between schools of social work and social agencies is seen most clearly in the field-instruction program. Both schools and agencies must open lines of communication, identify common goals and objectives, and make decisions that will enhance the quality of both social work education and social work practice. However, constraints exist within the agency that complicate the achievement of this complementary relationship. One constraint is that field practice is apt to be treated too casually by the agency and not viewed as part of the agency's service program. Agencies may not allocate sufficient resources to the field-instruction program to do the job adequately, and the role of the field instructor may not be as highly valued as it could be.[19] Agencies are responsible for identifying the importance of field instruction, for recognizing the merits of the field-instruction program, and for permitting the field instructor to meet the obligations of his or her role. Field instructors should feel that they are an integral part of the educational team, that they make a contribution not only to the student but to the agency, school, profession, and their own career. If field instructors are individualized within the agency, it is easier, in turn, for them to individualize the student. Field instructors must receive support from the agency if they are to function adequately in their teaching role. Such support also helps students realize their value as learners and potential professionals. In addition, agencies that stimulate their field instructors and other staff members to stretch themselves intellectually, whether through seminars, workshops, or other learning experiences, help students achieve balance among thinking, feeling, and doing, and support the notion that learning is an ongoing process.

THE FIELD INSTRUCTOR

Field instructors have a threefold responsibility: (1) teach social work effectively, (2) demonstrate professional skills, and (3) provide the support and learning experiences through which students can integrate social work knowledge, attitudes, and skills.

Teaching Social Work

A capable field instructor requires much more than having experienced field instruction as a student and a successful history of staff supervision or of being stimulated by new challenges. Skilled professional practitioners are not necessarily skilled educators, nor is it always easy for such persons to adapt to the academic world, especially when their primary commitment is to practice. Field instructors are often expected to shift roles from that of staff supervisor or practitioner to that of teacher. Little consideration may be given to what is involved in translating knowledge into the teaching experience and in developing competence in a variety of teaching methods. This shift from practitioner to field instructor, in the context of new practice demands, requires that field instructors broaden their repertoire and take risks to revamp their skills.[20] In addition, field instructors must be able to guide students through the beginning, middle, and ending phases of learning and respond to their capabilities as learners (see Chapter 2). Annette Garrett's early work on learning through field instruction describes and discusses students' learning tasks and phases in terms of the fall, winter, and spring periods of the academic year, and the relationship that is developed with the field instructor throughout the year.[21] Building and expanding a repertoire of teaching approaches and skills takes time, effort, and investment in professional development.

Although approaches to the teaching/learning process in the field-practice course may differ from those of the classroom, some comparisons can be made. For example in both the classroom and field practice, preparation is often time consuming; content must be understood not only for the field instructor's own knowledge and use but for the various ways it may be interpreted, understood, and used by others. Classroom content is focused on moving from the general to the specific, whereas in the practice experience the instructor must be ready to move quickly from one content area to another. If field instructors are not able to do so, they will be less helpful to students who are struggling to integrate their new knowledge with practice.

Demonstrating Professional Skill

Students look for a role model in their field instructor. They want to observe their instructor in action and to emulate him or her. Demonstration of skill is not as easy as it sounds. Field instructors must be ready to answer questions about their performance and to know the "whys" of their actions. Students expect them to be open and honest, to admit mistakes, and to accept challenges. Frequently, demands are made that are difficult to handle. Responding to such challenges requires a sensitivity to the reasons for the demands and a focus on the needs of the students.

Field instructors must develop a heightened awareness of what they are doing. Frequently, they are forced to rethink their approach or to realize that their thinking, feeling, and doing, are not in balance. Field instructors may feel exposed at such times and attempt to protect themselves. In such circumstances, caution must be taken lest focus remain on the field instructor rather than the learner.

Providing Support and Learning Experiences

Field instructors must be flexible with students and recognize that they are individuals who do not, cannot, and should not be expected to learn in the same way. Phillip Jackson emphasizes the importance of responding to the student's unique characteristics:

> Providing each student with his own tutor, or with an exclusive portion of his teacher's time, however, will not necessarily achieve the goal of individualization. The essential requirement is not that the teacher be alone with his

student but that he respond to the student's uniqueness with pedagogical wisdom. A teacher who is blind to the subtleties of the student's behavior, and who has a narrow repertoire of pedagogical alternatives on which to draw, cannot possibly individualize instruction in anything more than a superficial sense no matter how many hours he spends alone with his charge.[22]

Although it is expected that all students will have certain kinds of and multiple experiences during their field practice training, the timing will vary in accordance with the needs of the individual student (see Chapter 2).

Field instructors contribute a great deal to the learning atmosphere. Beginning students need help in identifying their strengths; they are fearful of making mistakes and need to feel supported before they are willing to take risks. Although field instructors must distinguish their role as educator from their primary role as therapist, they nevertheless use the same sustaining techniques with students as they do with their clients when initiating change. Students, like clients, are cautious in their approach to the unknown and want to hold on to what is comfortable. Field instructors must actively demonstrate their support. If students feel that their field instructors are concerned, interested, and involved in the teaching/learning process, they will find it easier to take risks and be challenged by the new ways of thinking, feeling, and doing that are required for professional development.

THE EDUCATIONAL INSTITUTION

The educational institution assumes a leadership role in making the essential connections among the school, student, and agency. It sets the overall objectives for the field-practice component and establishes the expected behaviors for students entering each level of professional practice according to the CSWE guidelines and the demands of the profession. Input from the practice community, including the consumers of service, is an essential part of the ongoing refinement of this process.

Educational institutions assume these responsibilities by assuring that the following items are inaugurated and implemented: (1) establish criteria for field practice; (2) schedule meetings, seminars, and workshops to aid in the integration process; (3) design guidelines for the selection and continual use of field-practice agencies; (4) establish a school liaison representative (advisor) with all parties involved in the educational endeavor; (5) provide a field work manual; and (6) set up a procedure for ongoing assessment and development of the field and academic program with agency administrators, field instructors, faculty, and students.

Criteria for Field Practice

Students and field instructors must clearly understand the expectations for the student in regard to pace and progress in learning. Educational institutions should develop criteria that will delineate the goals that students must achieve in relation to (1) the functioning of students within the agency and community; (2) direct work with the client system, including problem identification; collection, organization, and analysis of data; and selection, implementation, and evaluation of various interventions; (3) learning through field instruction and field experiences; (4) dealing with obstacles to learning; and (5) professional development. Such criteria provide direction to students in achieving their goals and provide the variables necessary for measuring performances. The 1974 *Report to the Task Force on Structure and Quality in Social Work Education* questioned whether the existing evaluative procedures are sufficiently rigorous.

> To build such measures of competence requires careful specification of performance objectives at each educational level, identification of the content to be covered and the appropriate learning experiences, and developing of measures to evaluate the outcome.[23]

If students and field instructors do not understand the established goals, learning may be frustrated, students' progress impeded, and evaluative procedures irrelevant (see Chapter 8).

Meetings, Seminars, and Workshops

The development of the field-instruction component of education depends in great measure on the increased competence and status of field instructors as educators. Provision for professional development of field instructors is needed for both the substance and method of teaching.[24] Schools should arrange meetings, seminars, and workshops for field instructors, which will help field instructors understand the curriculum design so as to coordinate classroom content and field practice and will stimulate further development of the knowledge and teaching skills that are required by the field instructors' assignments. Agencies can be relied upon to fulfill their responsibilities in the ongoing arrangement if the school establishes the expectations and provides the material and supports necessary to enable field instructors to be educators as well as competent practitioners. The process of synthesizing knowledge with practice skill can be accomplished if field instructors are informed about the theories that are being taught in various areas of the curriculum and if they are encouraged to emphasize the relevance of theory to current field assignments. Opportunities for ongoing learning and sharing give field instructors a sense of unity, belonging, and investment in the total educational program.

Selection and Continuation of Field-Practice Agencies

Schools should establish criteria for recruitment, acceptance, monitoring, and continuation of field-practice agencies and should inform agencies about what is involved in the placement of students. Agencies should be informed of the individual student's characteristics and experiences and should have the opportunity to participate in the selection of students. Schools should establish provisions for consultation. A written contractual agreement among school, agency, and student is becoming an accepted procedure. Schools are finding it necessary to guarantee that the rights and obligations of all parties are maintained and to ensure consistency in the learning experiences for students in field practice.

School Liaison Representatives

The sense of membership in the educational endeavor, not only for the field instructor but for the agency as a whole, can be strengthened through school representatives who consult with and advise the administrator, field instructor, and students in the field placement. Students' learning needs, progress, obstacles to learning, and the evaluation process as a means of assessing performance and establishing ongoing educational goals should be discussed. The changing needs of the agency, its resources, and its goals should also be discussed. The role of this educational consultant should be clearly defined, and the guidelines for consultation explicated (see Chapter 10).

Field-Work Manual

A comprehensive field-work manual is a good place to highlight the shared responsibilities of school, agency, and student. Review of its content and a regular exchange of information of mutual benefit to the school, agency, field instructor, and student should be done on an ongoing basis. Field instructors profit from hearing social work faculty discuss their course objectives, outlines, and teaching methodology. Providing a chance for field instructors to ask questions about the application of this content to the direct-practice experience enhances the quality of field teaching and strengthens the performance of field instructors as educators. Conversely, social work faculty can profit from hearing field instructors discuss agency practice, issues, and trends.

Assessment and Development of the Field and Academic Program

In addition to campus meetings, collaborative committee activity, and the educational consultant's visits to the agencies, schools should include field instructors and agency administrators in the ongoing assessment and development of the overall field and academic program. Seminars with field instructors, students, and faculty help develop the conviction that all parties have a contribution to make to social work education. Field instructors, agency administrators, and other agency representatives have expertise in a wide range of theory and practice areas. Schools should invite them to share this knowledge in special classes or programs. Schools have much to learn from the practice community, and avenues for exchange of information and experience should be built into the educational program.

THE STUDENT

Working with people who need help solving problems requires serious commitment on the part of students. They must be willing to involve themselves in the learning process; evaluate themselves throughout the experience; and change their ways of thinking, feeling, and doing. Although students learn in different ways and at varying rates, all must take responsibility for their own learning. In accepting placements at agencies, students contract with agencies that they will learn about and render services to the best of their abilities using appropriate resource systems. Learning through field instruction is a new experience for students and requires an openness and willingness to respond to suggestions and directions. Students must draw on their own knowledge base and test the validity of new knowledge and their capacity to intervene appropriately within various client, agency, and community systems.

The student's major responsibility is to meet the educational objectives established by the school. Criteria for a particular level of performance may specify the behaviors that students are expected to achieve: (1) learning about and functioning responsibly within the field-practice setting and community; (2) providing quality service to client systems in keeping with client needs and the student's level of knowledge and skill; (3) developing self-awareness and evaluating one's own performance; and (4) identifying with professional values, principles, and standards (see Chapters 8 and 9 on criteria for performance).

SUMMARY

Field-practice settings create an atmosphere for learning, provide a framework for learning organizational structure, present an arena for professional development, and offer educational support for students. Field instructors teach social work effectively, demonstrate professional skills, and provide the support and learning experiences through which students integrate social work knowledge, attitudes, and skills. Educational institutions provide a field-instruction manual and establish criteria for field practice. Meetings, seminars, and workshops are scheduled for field instructors to develop teaching skills and to add input into the curriculum design of the school. In addition, schools provide guidelines for selection and continued use of field-instruction agencies; establish a liaison representative with all parties involved; and set up procedures for ongoing assessment and development of the field and academic program with agency administrators, field instructors, faculty, and students. Students acquire and integrate knowledge of the concepts and principles of social work through direct experience with the service-delivery system. They develop skills in social work intervention with the client system and community in keeping with the various processes, roles, and competencies as delineated by the educational level of professional practice.

Based on the different nature and purposes of academic institutions and agencies, some tensions will persist in this partnership. The tensions can be minimized, however, if roles, responsibilities, and mutual benefits for the profession are clearly spelled out and each member of the partnership becomes an integral part of the education/practice process. Schools must make a more conscious effort to include agencies in the overall educational process. The educationally directed interplay among the school, agency, field instructor, and student must be viewed as a shared, reciprocal venture. An explicit design and sound framework that fosters a positive association with all parties engaged in the education of the social worker is needed to facilitate an effective program. If the educational institution is going to meet the goals articulated by CSWE and respond to the service-delivery systems of the 1980s and 1990s, a collaborative exchange of resources and a clearly defined procedural arrangement are of paramount importance.

REFERENCES

1. Margaret S. Schubert, "Curriculum Policy Dilemmas in Field Instruction," *Journal of Education for Social Work* 1 (Fall 1965): 35–46.

2. Helen Cassidy, "Role and Function of the Coordinator or Director of Field Instruction," in *Current Patterns in Field Instruction*, ed. Betty Lacy Jones (New York: Council on Social Work Education, 1969); and Ruppert A. Downing, "Bridging the Gap between Education and Practice," *Social Casework* 55 (June 1974): 352–59.

3. Carol H. Meyer, "Integrating Practice Demands in Social Work Education," *Social Casework* 49 (October 1968): 481–86.

4. Cassidy, "Role and Function of the Coordinator."

5. Margaret S. Schubert, "Making the Best Use of Traditional and Atypical Field Placements," in *Current Patterns in Field Instruction*, ed. Betty Lacy Jones (New York: Council on Social Work Education, 1969).

6. Sidney J. Berkowitz, "Agency-School Communications and Relationships: Redefinition of Agency-School Partnerships," *Social Work Education Reporter* 16 (December 1968): 59–69.

7. Harriet Bartlett, "Responsibilities of Social Work Practitioners and Educators toward Building a Strong Profession," *The Social Service Review* 34 (December 1960): 379–91.

8. Jerome Cohen, "Selected Constraints in the Relationship between Social Work Education and Practice," *Journal of Education for Social Workers* 13 (Winter 1977): 3–7.

9. Margaret L. Schutz and William E. Gordon, "Reallocation of Educational Responsibility among Schools, Agencies, Students and NASW," *Journal of Education for Social Work* 13 (Spring 1977): 99–106.

10. Katherine A. Kendall, *Reflections on Social Work Education 1950–1978* (New York: International Association of Schools of Social Work, 1978).

11. Francis Manis, *Openness in Social Work Field Instruction* (Goleta, Calif.: Kimberly Press, 1979).

12. Suanna J. Wilson, *Field Instruction: Techniques for Supervisors* (New York: The Free Press, 1981).

13. Bradford W. Sheafor and Lowell E. Jenkins, eds., *Quality Field Instruction in Social Work* (New York: Longman, 1982).

14. Max Siporin, "The Process of Field Instruction," in *Quality Field Instruction in Social Work*, ed. Bradford W. Sheafor and Lowell E. Jenkins (New York: Longman, 1982), pp. 175–97.

15. Jean M. Granger and Signe Starnes, *Field Instruction Model for Baccalaureate Social Work* (Syracuse, N.Y.: Syracuse University School of Social Work, 1982).

16. Elmer J. Tropman, "Agency Constraints Affecting Links between Practice and Education," *Journal of Education for Social Work* 13 (Winter 1977): 8–14.

17. Malcolm S. Knowles, *The Adult Learner: A Neglected Species* (Houston, Tex.: Gulf Publishing Company, 1973), p. 117.

18. Neilson F. Smith, "Practitioners' Orientations to Knowledge and Conceptual Learning from Practice: Part I," *Social Casework* 47 (October 1966): 507–14.

19. Kloh-Ann Amacher, "Explorations into the Dynamics of Learning in Field Work," *Smith College Studies in Social Work* 46 (June 1976): 163–217.

20. Susan Matorin, "Dimensions of Student Supervision: A Point of View," *Social Casework* 6 (March 1979): 150–56.

21. Annette Garrett, "Learning through Supervision," *Smith College Studies in Social Work* 24 (February 1954): 3–109.

22. Phillip Jackson, "Excerpt from *The Teacher and the Machine*," in *The Psychology of Open Teaching and Learning*, ed. Melvin L. Silberman, Jerome S. Allender, and Jay M. Yanoff (Boston: Little Brown and Company, 1972), p. 269.

23. Lillian Ripple, *Report to the Task Force on Structure and Quality in Social Work Education* (New York: Council on Social Work Education, August 1974), p. 49.

24. Jeanette Regensburg, "Report of Exploratory Project in Field Instruction," *Field Instruction in Graduate Social Work Education: Old Problems and New Proposals* (New York: Council on Social Work Education, 1966).

2

GUIDELINES FOR UNDERSTANDING THE PHASES OF LEARNING

> *Begin where the student is. . . . Accept and use whatever can be used of past experience to build upon for more learning. . . . Feed new learning as it can be assimilated and used.*
>
> —*Bertha Capen Reynolds*

Bertha Reynolds suggested five learning stages through which students progress as they face new experiences. These stages are as meaningful today as they were when she described them forty-five years ago.

Stage I: Acute consciousness of self. In this stage the learner feels unintelligent and unable to act. This period does not last long; eventually the learner finds security in responding appropriately to situations. The teacher's role is to help students develop a sense of personal adequacy and achieve success so that they have solid ground upon which to stand when subsequently they struggle with new experiences.

Stage II: Sink-or-swim adaptation. During this stage students struggle to keep up with situational demands and are likely to depend heavily on approval or disapproval from those with more experience. This stage may last longer. The teacher helps students gain security by mobilizing their existing knowledge and skills and encouraging them to trust and use their instinctive and spontaneous responses.

Stage III: Understanding the situation with little power to control one's activity in it. In this stage students have not yet developed a base of stabilized responses on which they can rely. The student understands what should be done but is very uneven in his or her ability to respond appropriately. Students may remain in this stage a long time, perhaps even years, before they achieve relative mastery of their profession. The teacher should help students admit mistakes without loss of courage and emphasize partial successes.

Stage IV: Relative mastery. In this stage, students are able to understand and control their activity in the profession. Conscious intelligence and unconscious responses are integrated. The teacher should continue to stimulate the learner lest he or she become smug and forget that situations do not repeat themselves and that new challenges must be mastered.

Stage V: Teaching what one has mastered. In this stage the social worker is able to teach others. Even in this stage, however, the teacher needs guidance and encouragement as much as the student. The teacher needs feedback about the effectiveness of his or her efforts so that the entire learning process may be viewed with perspective.[1]

Since students do not complete stages four and five during their years of formal education, the present chapter discusses the needs of students during the beginning, middle, and ending phases of field practice, which are comparable to Reynolds's first three stages. Social work practice emphasizes the importance of evaluating the beginning, middle, and end of intervention; field instructors also will find it valuable to focus on the needs and achievements of students during these phases of learning. Guidelines are suggested for helping field instructors instruct and guide social work students through these phases of learning, including ways in which students may be made aware of learning phases and deal with the tasks involved. Learning phases can be adapted to all levels of student learning, be it undergraduate or first- or second-level graduate. Emphasis and timing will vary; for example, the beginning phase may require greater emphasis and thus last longer with undergraduate and first-level graduate students, whereas second-level graduate students may move quickly into the middle phase. The ending phase has an added importance for undergraduate and second-level graduate students in that both are terminating involvement with the educational system and the field placement.

THE BEGINNING PHASE

Structure and support are critical in the beginning phase of field-practice learning. Students are often bewildered when they make the transition from classroom learning to field practice, as they move from words and ideas to face the special demands of involvement with people.[2] An awareness of students' initial responses to these demands helps in identifying their level of anxiety and in determining ways to alleviate their anxiety. Assessing learning, therefore, should begin immediately so that students' strengths can be utilized and problem areas identified.

Initial Responses to Learning

Ordinarily, students begin their field practice with a high level of anxiety, which manifests itself in various ways. Students' expectations in the beginning phase are vague and often global, even when they have carefully read the learning expectations that are identified in the field-instruction manual or have discussed these expectations during orientation sessions. They think that some magic formula can and must be found. Students at the second level of graduate education are afraid that they may not know enough and wonder if they will be able to meet the higher level of expectations. Their confidence wanes as they wonder whether they will be able to translate what they have learned to the new agency and client systems. Students must learn how the agency operates, the kinds of services offered, the various roles of the social worker, and the specific tasks that they will be expected to perform. A large complex setting can be overwhelming for students, and they may feel that they must learn everything at once.

Field instructors must be aware of the individual student's anxiety level. All students need reassurance that they cannot and need not learn everything at once, nor should they be expected to link clients with services without explicit direction and opportunities for trial and error. Information about agency operations and community resources should be repeated, depending on the students' ability to absorb this information. Observing the students' level of anxiety also helps field instructors to select and time client assignments. Field instructors should attempt to provide opportunities for students to draw from prior experiences; determine the usefulness of these experiences; and test new knowledge in relation to agency policies, procedures, and services.

Observational Experiences

Observational experiences enable students to see clients and the professional worker interacting in the helping process (see Chapter 3). These experiences force students to observe behavior and challenge them to assess intervention skills and make connections with their own newly acquired knowledge. Student–instructor discussions about the observational experience enable students to draw comfortably on their prior experiences and allow both student and instructor to identify strengths early in the semester.

This idea was taken several steps further in an innovative model for training family therapists through direct observation and supervision of the trainee. In this model, one student interviews while another student and the supervisor observe behind a one-way mirror. The supervisor has three alternatives for directing a trainee: He or she may telephone, convene a brief conference outside the training interview, or enter the training interview. Before and after the training interview, brief teaching and planning sessions are held. Field instructors gain a clearer picture of the individual student's ability to implement theoretical knowledge and freedom to question and share ideas.[3] By initiating field practice with observational experiences, field instructors are better able to assign tasks that gradually involve students in more independent practice and that allow them to master professional skills and to experience success.

Role Play

Role play with students can be effectively used in all three learning phases. In the beginning phase it helps students prepare for first interviews, especially when they are experiencing anxiety. Ordinarily students express apprehension about initial client reaction. Ten to fifteen minutes, perhaps less, is often sufficient to relieve students' fear that they will be unable to utter a word or that the client will observe their nervousness. Reversing roles also helps students understand what the client might be going through.

Some field instructors routinely take students through a first interview in which the field instructor assumes the role of a typical client served by the agency. The student completes a process recording, which is discussed later with the field instructor. The field instructor, in turn, shares his or her impressions, both as a client and as a teacher; particular emphasis is placed on reinforcing the positive aspects of the interview and the strengths of the student. (See Appendix C for a role-play recording and comments of a student and field instructor.) Many students who have undergone this exercise have commented on the ease with which both assume their respective roles; discomfort is quickly replaced by natural involvement in the situation. Although the process recording may feel threatening to students, it can also be challenging and rewarding. Students have stated that the benefits outweigh the discomfort involved.

Assessing Learning

Evaluating students prior to the middle phase of learning allows field instructors and students to become familiar with the areas being assessed and to identify beginning progress in the acquisition of knowledge, attitudes, and skills in those areas. In addition to the evaluative feedback included in field-instruction conferences, other processes may be required to consolidate learning and practice skills. An informal midsemester evaluation can help in reviewing learning to date and in developing a mutual focus for future learning. When one has been through this evaluatory process and experienced its usefulness, the end-of-the-semester evaluation is often viewed with less apprehension.[4] Because students learn at different rates, unevenness in performance is evident at this time. It is important, therefore, for both student and field instructor to review what the student brought to the experience in terms of strengths, limitations, and life experiences as well as how the student has been able to use and develop this background.

Obstacles to Learning

Some obstacles to learning usually are evident and discussed prior to the evaluation. However, their effect on the total performance may not be identified clearly until the first formal evaluation. The new awareness may mark a turning point in the learning/doing process, and the students may be better prepared to engage in constructive ways of working through learning difficulties. Charlotte Towle says of the student who learns through difficulties:

> The distinctive characteristic of the productive learner is not that he is defenseless but that his defenses, by and large, in mitigating the conflicts activated by learning permit him to confront them and to have an educative and often also a corrective experience.[5]

It is extremely important, therefore, that students are aware of their pace and progress early in their learning experience so that required goals can be achieved by the end of the placement.

MIDDLE PHASE

In the middle phase of the students' learning, their anxiety level is lower and the fruits of learning are beginning to emerge. Students become aware of these changes, and pieces of the puzzle begin to fit together for them. They begin to feel excited about the learning process and experience some success in their interventions with clients. Students begin to take more responsibility in the learning process, although at times they may still need to be stimulated to do so.

Field instructors must be prepared to help students become involved in evaluating their own performance. This can be accomplished through the use of written and taped recordings, through their preparation for conferences, and through the atmosphere for learning provided by their field instructors. Proper use of these teaching tools helps promote self-awareness and more autonomous functioning.

The Written Recording

The use of process recording can be an extremely helpful tool in the learning/teaching process. It can lead to precise discussions about the content of interviews, as opposed to sweeping generalities and conclusions by students about their findings. It allows the field instructor to teach interviewing techniques based on the student's contact with the client rather than on abstractions. Ultimately, process recording can become an active learning tool for the students as they analyze their own process.[6] The more advanced students are able to criticize their own work by making margin notes or by identifying interviewing techniques that they have used.[7] The ability of students to criticize their own work through a written recording helps identify those students who have made the transition from the beginning to the middle phase of learning. Even graduate students who are in their second field placement are cautious in self-criticism and desire some comfort in the student–field instructor relationship before risking self-exposure. Thus written recording works as a springboard for focusing more clearly on many facets of student learning. How it is used in teaching should relate directly to what the student is expected to achieve; this expectation should be understood by both the field instructor and student.

Audiotapes and Role Playing

Audiotapes for recording interviews are an excellent teaching/learning tool for students in the middle phase of the learning process. Audiotapes are not recommended for students in the beginning phase; they are more self-protective and are only beginning to expose themselves to risk. Initially, tapes may be used by the student only and need not be shared with the field instructor. In the middle phase, students are clearer about learning goals and beginning to feel some progress is being made toward achieving these goals. Despite their apparent readiness to tape interviews, however, students may feel threatened by this new experience. Preparing students is important; they should be reassured that such feelings are normal. Anxiety can be allayed by permitting students considerable freedom in the selection of their client(s) for taping interviews and encouraging them to tape a series of interviews with the same client in order to become comfortable with the method. Helping students anticipate the client's feelings and reactions to being recorded will help students shift their focus from their own anxieties to the client's concerns about recording and confidentiality.

The audiotape is not the only item that should be discussed during conferences. Students should be prepared with written material that includes a statement of the purpose of the interview, observations of the client, and an assessment of the interview. The assessment should incorporate students' awareness of techniques used, evidence of progress related to intervention goals, areas of client concern that were not recognized and lack of follow-through on the part of the student, skills and techniques that will need to be developed, and ideas about how to proceed with the client.

The major advantage in using an audio recording as a learning tool is the objectivity it introduces for both students and field instructors; that is, it helps students become more aware of their clients and themselves in the interviews as well as overcome evasions, distortions, and other defenses. The nonverbal dimensions of the interview, such as tone of voice, inflections, and pauses, are also highlighted on the audiotape. Moreover, discussing the audiotape introduces subtle changes in the relationship between the student and the field instructor. The student is forced to face him- or herself rather than the supervisor's definition of him or her.[8] The objective evidence is there and students cannot escape; thus they are forced to be more objective in the critique of their own performance. The major disadvantage of the audiotape is the time involved, particularly for the field instructor. This can be controlled somewhat by limiting the number of taped interviews that are used for teaching purposes.

Video equipment adds another dimension to the teaching/learning experience in that facial expressions, body movement, and so forth can be viewed and discussed. Students should gather the same written materials as were described for audio recording when preparing for the evaluation.

By the end of the middle phase of learning, students are more comfortable in the agency setting and with the field instructor. They are more clear about their learning needs, more creative in their use of self, and more willing to take risks. Initiating role-play experiences at this time can help students achieve a different focus in order to work through blocks in both client progress and student learning.

Self-Awareness

During the middle phase of learning, students must deal with the need to achieve increased self-awareness (see Chapter 3). As they become more aware of their need to change ways of thinking, feeling, and doing, students may resist by clinging to more comfortable ways of responding to people, problems, and issues. They feel stilted when they use new behaviors, although they are rewarded when they experience success with the expanded use of self. Field instructors must assist students over this hurdle by helping them find their strengths and "place" as practitioners. Field instructors should be aware of alternative methods to helping students overcome their resistance to change and of the importance of involving others in the agency or the school to help each student progress and integrate change.

ENDING PHASE

Students must deal with feelings of separation and may experience regression and resistance when making this transition in the learning process. Students' reactions and needs vary, depending on whether they are completing their first field-practice experience or their involvement with the entire educational program. During this learning phase the field instructor should help students terminate involvement with clients, the agency, and, in some situations, the educational system.

Completing the First Field-Practice Experience

Students who are completing their first field-practice experience must deal with their issues of separation and loss, successes and failures with clients, and the knowledge they have gained or not gained over an extended period of time. The ending phase of the helping relationship in social work has been referred to as a neglected dimension. Similarly, the ending phase of learning may also suffer from neglect due to the demands on students to complete their class and field assignments and to prepare for examinations and employment. In addition, continuing students must focus on new beginnings in different agencies, with different field instructors and added expectations.

Field instructors must be aware of the many behaviors that may be precipitated by these transitions. They should help students become aware of the feelings that they are experiencing and assure students that such feelings are not unique. These feelings are growth producing and should be viewed as a normal reaction to ending an important phase of learning on the one hand and of beginning a new phase of learning on the other hand. The final evaluation helps students to look objectively at their progress throughout the practice course, the content of their experience, their strengths, and the areas that require continued development. As Charlotte Towle so aptly states:

> Having experienced a helping process in which he has survived stresses, in large part because he sought and took help, it is hoped that his respect for the recipient of help will be deepened. Having experienced frustration through his own limitations and through the limitations of his profession in society, in the context of the relationship that has eased the trauma, it is hoped that he will go forth with increased capacity to lose without losing.[9]

Completing the Educational Program

For many students the ending phase marks their separation from formal academic life and entails a drastic change in life-style. Students may feel pressure from the pending responsibility of professional employment or from the need to make a decision about graduate education. Selecting a different career goal might be in order for the undergraduate student. Graduate and undergraduate students who seek employment in the field find that their energies begin to shift toward thinking and planning for the right position within the profession, concerns about how to present themselves, and the problems they will encounter in the competitive job market. For many students, separation from their field instructors and the agencies where their relationships have at last been clarified, might result in sudden dependency and perhaps anger at the realization of losing these important supports. A study of students' experiences with the termination phase of individual treatment identified considerable uncertainty among students about their future. Many students reported that they had already disengaged from their clients and that their primary anxieties now concerned finishing their course assignments and finding work. They had mixed feelings about leaving school, and some found the idea of giving up their protected status as students frightening.[10]

During the ending phase the school must play a more active role with students. Educational advisors should be directly involved in helping students make the transition to graduate education, the work world, and the realities of employment opportunities. Students should be sufficiently comfortable with their advisors to be able to discuss their fears of leaving the security of the academic institution and dealing with another new experience. This extremely important service is frequently overlooked by the educational institution because of the demands and stresses that occur at the end of the academic year.

SUMMARY

Graduate and undergraduate students deal with varying levels of stress during the beginning, middle, and ending phases of learning in their respective field placements. Undergraduates and first-level graduate students tend to spend a longer time in the beginning phase, whereas graduate students in their second field placements may move more quickly into the middle phase. Field instructors must help students deal with the tasks of each phase. Beginning-phase tasks include reduction of anxiety, achieving comfort within the field placement and the community, and testing the use of self within the client system. In the middle phase, theory must merge with practice; ways of thinking, feeling, and doing must change to accommodate growth. Obstacles to learning and a plan for working on these problems should be identified. In the ending phase, students must understand their progress, strengths, and areas for continued growth.

Field instructors should be aware of the pressures and behaviors inherent in these phases and respond with appropriate teaching techniques that will move students through the three phases of learning and toward becoming competent practitioners. A clearly defined, structured approach to learning and assessment of students' anxiety level and prior experiences are important teaching guides in the first phase of learning. Observational experiences, role play, and individual attention to assignments are effective teaching techniques during the early weeks of field placement. Written recordings, audiotapes, individual and group conferences, and variety in assignments are valuable teaching components during the middle phase of learning. Conscious attempts to help students integrate theoretical content with practice skill should also be encouraged during the middle phase, and field instructors should be aware of the student's changing patterns of thinking, feeling, and doing. Field instructors should help students review progress, evaluate professional growth, and engage in career planning. The school, through the educational advisor system, should play an active role in helping students separate from the academic institution, enter into the next educational level, or enter the work world.

Field instruction requires an understanding of the learning expectations at particular educational levels, the experiences and talents students bring to the learning process, and ways in which students can be helped to use and develop their strengths.

> To study learners to see what they bring to the learning experience and how they change in it, as a group as well as individually in contact with the social forces playing upon them, calls for all the conscious intelligence we have as teachers and supervisors of field practice.[11]

This requires thought and preparation on the part of the field instructor and an ability to differentiate among teaching approaches.

REFERENCES

1. Bertha C. Reynolds, *Learning and Teaching in the Practice of Social Work* (New York: Russell & Russell, 1965).

2. Francis Manis, *Field Practice in Social Work Education: Perspectives from an International Base* (Fullerton, Calif.: Sultana Press, 1972), p. 95.

3. Vernon C. Rickert and John E. Turner, "Through the Looking Glass: Supervision in Family Therapy," *Social Casework* 59 (March 1978): 131–37.

4. Alex Gitterman and Naomi Pines Gitterman, "Social Work Student Evaluation: Format and Method," *Journal of Education for Social Work* 15 (Fall 1979): 103–108.

5. Charlotte Towle, *The Learner in Education for the Professions* (Chicago: The University of Chicago Press, 1954).

6. Esther Urdang, "In Defense of Process Recording," *Smith College Studies in Social Work* 50 (November 1979): 1–15.

7. Suanna J. Wilson, *Recording: Guidelines for Social Workers* (New York: The Free Press, 1980).

8. Frank Itzin, "The Use of Tape Recording in Field Work," *Social Casework* 41 (April 1960): 197–202.

9. Towle, *The Learner in Education*, p. 174.

10. Robert Paul Gould, "Students' Experience with the Termination Phase of Individual Treatment," *Smith College Studies in Social Work* 48 (June 1978): 235–69.

11. Reynolds, *Learning and Teaching*, p. 85.

3

INDIVIDUALIZING THE LEARNER

There is no such thing as a typical or an average social work student. Any illusion that there is rests on ignorance of the student.

—*Annette Garrett*

Students learn at different rates; their readiness to learn is an important factor in the learning process. Although all students are required to meet certain criteria within a specified time, it is possible to maximize learning and thus achieve educational and practice goals more effectively by establishing a sound curriculum and policy and by collaborative planning on the part of all involved — the school, agency, field instructor, and student.

Schools must be clear and explicit about the kinds and amount of field-practice experience in which students should be involved. These experiences should be introduced in accordance with the student's individual learning needs and based on what the student brings to the experience: theoretical and practice preparation, motivation, maturity, level of anxiety, and ability to handle new situations. Field-practice agencies must be ready to meet students' needs through the provision of client, community, and agency experience as well as a qualified field instructor who is willing to assume a teaching role. The nature of the students' tasks, the way they are selected, and their place in the educational scheme can either free or block learning. There are, however, handicaps involved in selecting tasks for students, one of which is the conflict between the primary objective of the agency to render services and the primary objective of the educational institution to educate the student.[1] Both can be achieved if the placements give ample time to the acculturation of students and provide a climate that permits students to act on their commitments, express their attitudes, and play out their roles. Only then can instructors and students focus on the students' responsibility to contribute direct-practice input into the system and to understand the interrelatedness of the units involved in the teaching/learning system.[2] Within such a milieu, maximal student learning can be achieved through the instructor understanding the adult learner, selecting the appropriate learning experience, promoting integration of theory with practice, helping the student develop self-awareness, and assuring active participation in evaluation.

THE ADULT LEARNER

Malcolm Knowles refers to certain conditions for learning and links these with teaching principles.
- Learners feel a need to learn.
- The learning environment is characterized by physical comfort, mutual trust and respect, mutual helpfulness, freedom of expression, and acceptance of differences.
- Learners perceive the goals of a learning experience as their own goals.
- Learners accept a share of the responsibility for planning and operating a learning experience and therefore have a feeling of commitment toward it.
- Learners participate actively in the learning process.
- The learning process is related to and makes use of the experience of the learners.
- Learners sense progress toward their goals.[3]

Unless these conditions are met, the tutorial approach used in field instruction is of little value.

The relationship between adult learning and social work practice was further emphasized by Hazel G. Price. Both adult learning and social work practice emphasize socially interdependent needs of individuals and the importance of affording all persons the opportunity to actualize their highest potential. Both require the following:
- Establishing a working climate that has structure but does not emphasize formality
- Assessing needs and interests with all parties involved before putting a plan into action
- Arriving at a mutual understanding before focusing on a specific objective
- Guiding the focus and work toward the agreed-upon goals and objectives
- Supporting a system of feedback and the democratic process[4]

The teaching/learning process in social work education has also been compared with the functioning of a railway system, wherein various situations, roles, functions, processes, and interactions are involved. The student is seen as the train, the engineer, and the conductor, whereas the teacher is the dispatcher who knows the various routes and who can guide, signal, and alert when necessary.[5] The engineer and conductor must, of course, know how to interpret the various signals and guidelines and must be included in the overall planning of the destination to be reached.

Adult learners, too, must participate in the structuring of their own learning experiences; the tutorial approach is a good way to meet this need, although there are problems inherent in this method. It may reactivate earlier problems with authority and dependency in students. The extent to which such problems persist depends on the field instructor's ability to individualize the learner and to deal with the transference and countertransference elements involved. Some dependency is part of the learning process, especially in the beginning phase; timing appropriate changes in method is important in helping students move toward greater autonomy in their practice functioning.

SELECTION OF LEARNING EXPERIENCES

The kinds and number of experiences must be selected carefully for each student. The school will generalize these expectations for learning, but field instructors must begin to individualize their students immediately in terms of readiness for client contacts, the kind of client (individual, family, group, community) for the student's initial contact, and the number of such assignments the student might be able to handle *vis-à-vis* current learning needs. Bernece Simon suggests several important considerations when designing learning experiences for students: (1) how to ensure a minimum equality of learning opportunities for all students, regardless of their field placements or field instructors, (2) how to achieve orderly learning in a disorderly situation or how to relate the "life order" of the field to the logical order of organized knowledge, and (3) how to contribute to the student's development toward professional independence. This design of learning experiences must be undergirded with solid content and related to teaching methods appropriate to the intent of the learning experiences.[6]

Identifying Learning Experiences

In order to facilitate learning and help students utilize their full potential, the following cognitive, affective, and active learning experiences are suggested:

- Orientation to the agency and community: information about agency policies, procedures, and the rationale for them; history; mission; relationship to and interaction with the community
- Opportunity to participate in agency functions, that is, staff meetings, consultations, unit meetings, conferences, and so forth
- Handle tasks of gradually increasing complexity; function as a member of the service delivery team with clearly delineated tasks in direct or indirect services delivery, then gradually move into total responsibility for providing helping services to clients.
- Opportunity to be involved in direct services to clients of varying ethnic, racial, and religious backgrounds
- Experience in fact-gathering, analyzing, and assessing situations, identifying the intervention needed, and working toward client and social systems change
- Obtain experience with various interventive modes, utilize community resources in conjunction with the agency, and collaborate with other disciplines to meet the needs of clients
- Prepare and use various kinds of recordings for learning/teaching and agency purposes
- Individualize experience for professional self-development; provide a base for students to identify with the values and purposes of the profession and provide support to enable students to deal with their own changes in ways of thinking, feeling, and doing
- Participate in the evaluation process as a means of learning to assess practice objectively and develop disciplined use of self

Learning tasks must have a valid rationale and must be based on sound service, teaching, and learning principles. All these give a coherent order to the teaching/learning process.[7] These experiences, however, are meaningless unless students are individualized as learners and unless the field-instruction component consciously promotes students' integration of theory and development of self-awareness.

Student Readiness to Engage in Learning Experiences

Undergraduate students begin their field practice after they complete many of their required social work courses and the majority of their core courses. Most, if not all, undergraduate programs require students to have a volunteer experience in a service-connected program prior to their field-practice course. However, many have had no work experience in a social agency. Consequently, learning in the field is often a new experience for baccalaureate students and requires a shift in their approach to learning. Undergraduate students are interested in doing and want immediate activity with clients. They frequently forget classroom learning; uppermost in their minds is the desire to do all things for all people. It takes patience and skill on the part of the field instructor to encourage students to move more slowly, take one step at a time, and bring their thinking into a better balance with their doing.

Graduate students come with a variety of life and employment experiences. Many have tested their skills, have achieved a sense of identity in the profession, and are clear about their goals. They usually begin with more confidence in their ability to work with clients; however, they may feel threatened in the practice experience by the fear that they will be unable to meet expectations or that they must unlearn their ways of approaching and working with clients. These fears may be intensified with the emphasis on developing conscious awareness of use of self and the importance of making the necessary changes in their accustomed ways of thinking, feeling, and doing.

Past experiences and prior successes should be discussed with students regardless of their level of learning so that they do not feel inadequate. Helping students identify their strengths in the beginning of their field practice and showing ways they can operationalize these strengths will build confidence and lessen feelings of inadequacy. Sharing positive experiences that highlight their abilities and discussing areas of learning already achieved can help students become less self-protective about their lack of knowledge. Also, students feel more free to take risks and to make productive use of their field instructors.

An Agency and Community Experience

Early in their field course, students should be required to study their field-instruction setting and the community in which it is located. This assignment should be completed and evaluated by the school or field instructor at a designated time, that is, sometime around mid-semester. This assignment has been used successfully with undergraduate students and is a valuable learning opportunity for graduate students as well.

Purpose. Conducting a study of the field-instruction setting helps students become comfortable with and learn some of the specifics of their field placements, that is, the structure and characteristics of the communities in which they are placed. This assignment is especially appropriate for students who are placed in large metropolitan areas.

Value. Studying the placement setting helps students appreciate the complexities of the various systems with which they will be dealing and begin to integrate theoretical components with their factual and impressionistic findings. More specifically, studying the placement setting will

1. help students become comfortable moving around the geographic area and help them establish professional relationships in the community;
2. provide an opportunity for students to work collaboratively with peers in planning, organizing, and participating in the study;
3. help students develop an awareness of the uniqueness of the community through the collection of factual and impressionistic material and the selection of appropriate information that will lead to understanding the relationship of agency services with the community needs;
4. broaden the student's understanding of community services, gaps in services, how individuals and families are affected, and how agencies offering services affect each other; and
5. provide the student with an orientation to the field agency as a social system, and examine some of the characteristics of this system and transactions with other environmental systems.

Observational Experiences

Client–worker observational experiences are helpful during the early phase of learning for the undergraduate and first-level graduate students. These experiences might be introduced before the students' client contacts or simultaneously with their first assigned client.

Value for the student. Observational experiences allow students to test their feelings, reactions, and knowledge base in an actual client situation without the pressure of being a "worker" who is being evaluated. It permits students to see how workers handle critiques of their performance and how they share their thoughts and feelings with others. Students learn that a client situation may be approached in a variety of ways and may begin to identify with the professional worker who acts as a model for performance. Students can transfer this experience quite readily to their own client contacts.

Value for the field instructor. Observational experiences provide another way for field instructors to individualize the student. They can note the student's willingness to take risks during discussions and signs of integrating classroom theory with field practice. Field instructors are able to observe the student's level of anxiety and begin planning ways to reduce anxiety by promoting successful experiences for the student. Field instructors will obtain a better idea of the kinds and amount of experience the student needs to feel successful.

INTEGRATION OF THEORY AND PRACTICE

Social work education should be an integrative experience; that is, the student should be consistently challenged and helped to see the parts in relation to the whole and the connections between means and ends. The integrative process takes longer for some students, especially at the undergraduate level. Field instructors need to guide actively all students to make appropriate connections between practice and their values and knowledge base.

Student Readiness

Undergraduate students are usually eager to make use of their theoretical knowledge in the initial phase of field practice, especially if the first experiences are observational (agency, community, group, or client). However, as students begin to take more responsibility for direct client contacts, they must become comfortable in this activity and their primary efforts begin to move in that direction. Consequently, regression rather than progression in learning may be noted. The need for students to experience comfort with the "old self" in a new experience is extremely important and should not be confused with a lack of progress or problems in learning. Readiness to move forward depends on students' ability to feel success in "doing" even though they may be unable to identify reasons for the success or to connect theory with doing. As students become more comfortable with themselves as human services professionals, they begin to make changes in ways of thinking, feeling, and doing and to move from intuitive responses to a conscious evaluation of self and client. Second-level graduate students may also experience a period of regression in the early phase of their second field-practice placement and may need time and help to connect and integrate past learning into a new setting where the demands appear overwhelming.

Need for Guidelines

It is easy for students to become complacent and not integrate theory with practice. Students at this point can profit from explicit guidelines on how to integrate their new knowledge. Process recording reflects the extent to which students are making reference to new knowledge and developing a conscious use of self. The field instructor may need to direct the individual student to be more specific in certain areas of the recording. It may be helpful also to students if they are required to identify what is currently being discussed in the various classroom courses and to review the outlines of courses that have been completed or experiences that have been mastered with the field instructor. The field instructor should not hesitate to suggest specific readings to students that are appropriate to their case situations; this assignment should be followed by a discussion of the content. In certain instances, students should be asked to rewrite a specific section of the recording in order to incorporate new knowledge.

Results of Integration
Students at all levels of field practice feel some discomfort as they are pushed to incorporate thinking with doing; however, they feel satisfaction as they experience success. Success stimulates students to take risks, combine the old with the new, and make necessary changes. It is an incentive to be more creative and more clear about the additional knowledge they must acquire and to set goals accordingly. It moves students toward the realization that skill in the use of knowledge is the most important skill of all.[8]

SELF-AWARENESS

Self-awareness is an important component in social work education. Without it, students are not amenable to change and cannot develop effective use of self. Self-awareness cannot be taught solely through an intellectual process; it requires the emotional experience usually encountered in field practice.

Tasks for the Student
Students who enter a social work educational program must become sufficiently clear about their goals and establish priorities in relation to achieving these goals. The demands are particularly stressful for older students with both family and job responsibilities. To develop self-awareness, students must accept themselves in the dual roles of student and worker and do so without excessive anxiety or resorting to infantile defenses. Students must be able to shift to a professional self-image and expose themselves to risk in achieving this image. Risk involves being flexible with clients; openness in discussions with the field instructor; and freedom to express reactions, feelings, and ideas in written recordings. A basic task that cuts across the learning experience is the acceptance and use of constructive criticism from others and the criticizing of

one's own performance. Accepting criticism and self-criticizing involve the student in the learning process and permit him or her to deal with obstacles that impede progress.

Role of the Field Instructor
Field instructors play a key role in helping students develop self-awareness. In an exploratory study of the role self-awareness plays in the learning process of first-level graduate social work students, it was concluded that field instruction was an important source for the development of self-awareness. During the learning process, students feel a need to please the instructor, take on the personality of the instructor, and seek reassurance.[9] The relationship between the student and the field instructor involves an awareness of transference and countertransference elements while maintaining the focus on learning. The field instructor supports the student so that the student's anxiety is sufficiently low to permit self-examination and prevent healthy curiosity from being blocked. The field instructor must carefully evaluate disturbances in the student's capacity to develop self-awareness and must determine the degree to which these disturbances interfere with learning. Field instructors must help students increase their capacity for self-awareness or decide if the disturbances are beyond the scope of field instruction.

Establishing a Base of Comfort
Most students need to experience success before testing their new knowledge and risking themselves with clients, field instructors, or in their field placements. Students' initial success is directly related to their identified strengths and the opportunity to use these strengths within a range of experiences. After the base of comfort has been established, students are much more willing to look at areas that need to be developed or changed. However, before students are able to identify the areas that need to be developed or changed and before they are willing to initiate change, they must become conscious of how they respond to clients. Process recording is a helpful tool in identifying areas that need to be developed. Guiding students to make necessary changes requires considerable skill on the part of the field instructor. Students must be allowed to discuss their anxieties and fears about doing things differently or moving to a deeper level of understanding. They may resist by challenging the value and probable success of the change or by requiring time to mull it over. Other students may attempt to please the field instructor and find it difficult to discuss their dis-

comfort. Field instructors should be prepared for a variety of student reactions to change.

Anticipating Reactions

Students should be prepared for some of the reactions and feelings they will experience in learning about self. They will make discoveries that may be gratifying or anxiety provoking. One of the most painful areas of self-awareness for young, inexperienced students who often wish to "rescue all their clients" is the sudden awareness of their own prejudices and stereotypes regarding people and behavior and that their clients are responding to their real feelings. Students can shift from feeling a sense of omnipotence and omniscience to a sense of impotency and inadequacy, which is a painful experience that requires support from the field instructor. Field instructors must be sensitive to students' reactions to client, agency, and peer situations. No matter how blatant their reactions may be, it may be difficult for students to acknowledge some of their reactions. Reactions and responses in the field setting do not necessarily come out in the classroom. The field setting, however, provides the opportunity for students to make necessary changes in perceptions, attitudes, and approaches. If students are supported by their field instructor and others in their placement setting, they are better able to perceive themselves objectively and to expose themselves to risk in ongoing client, agency, and community activities.

Self-Criticism

Students should be encouraged to criticize their own work. It is much easier and more rewarding for students if they identify concerns or areas in the field experience that might have been approached differently before the field instructor does so. The field instructor is then able to recognize the student's strength in being able to identify weaknesses rather than emphasizing what should or might have been done. Self-criticism can be promoted through written recordings, tapes, role play, discussions in conferences, and group process within the field setting. Perhaps the most crucial time for self-criticism is during evaluations.

STUDENT EVALUATION

Informal Evaluation

Student evaluation is an ongoing process that begins when students arrive at their field placement. Informally, it is part of every student–field instructor conference. If field instructors clarify their expectations for students, surprises will be avoided during formal evaluation conferences.

Formal Evaluation

The formal evaluation at the end of an academic period sums up and pulls together the progress that has been achieved by the student. This in itself is an effective learning experience for students. In addition to reviewing students' progress in learning, the formal evaluation provides an opportunity for students and field instructors to share ideas, clarify issues concerning learning and teaching, and formulate together an educational plan for the future. The formal evaluation highlights and examines the learning process; it requires effort and planning. The evaluation conference should be presented from two vantage points: students' learning progress and the role of field instruction in this endeavor.

Preparation for Evaluation

Early discussions. Early in their placements, students are concerned about how they will be graded. The field-practice evaluation process is a new experience for most undergraduate and some first-level graduate students; in no way does it resemble the grading procedures of the classroom. Discussion of this approach to evaluating learning should take place early in the placement. It should be presented initially by the school, and the evaluation procedure and its contribution to the learning experience should be reemphasized later by the field instructor. The more explicitly the evaluation process is discussed, the easier it is to avoid such statements as "nobody ever told me" or "if I had known, my performance would have been different."

Review of conference content. Student conferences should be structured so that expectations, achievements, and areas needing improvement are understood by the student. Field instructors and students should keep notes on each conference. Notes may be as simple as merely jotting down the strengths and difficulties that were emphasized and the areas to be strengthened between conferences. This procedure not only helps in planning ongoing conferences but is an excellent source in reviewing learning when preparing for the formal evaluation.

Review of recordings. Reviewing process recording is another excellent way to prepare for the formal evaluation conference (see Chapter 5 for discussion of process recordings). The process recording is probably the most important evidence of learning, and the review helps both students and field instructors rethink what students brought to the field-placement experience and examine students' application of new knowledge, attitudes, and skills. Review of the process recording helps identify the extent of integration of classroom content and readings with practice as well as the specific areas that need further work. Reviewing other forms of written communication, for example, letters, referrals, and summaries, also helps students assess their own needs and stimulates field instructors to increase the amount and variety of learning opportunities.

Written preparation. Criteria for performance for each semester should be made available to students at the beginning of the field-practice courses. Prior to the evaluation, students should study this material and relate the expectations to their own performance. Students should prepare written material using the instrument designed by the school, which should then be shared with field instructors just as field instructors' written materials are shared with students. Making comparisons and discussing differences can be a learning experience for both. If a difference of opinion cannot be negotiated, each has the right to include a statement that clarifies his or her particular point of view in the written evaluation submitted to the school. Thus students are taught to base their learning assessment on the facts and to present clear documentation of their learning experience.

Working Out Problems

From the prepared written materials, students and field instructors can identify areas of learning that need to be developed, areas that have been neglected, and areas that require change. The future learning goals should be arrived at jointly and should be reasonable and attainable. If learning problems have arisen during the semester, they should be clearly documented in the evaluation together with procedures that will help the student deal with the problem(s) and the progress made thus far (see Chapter 11 for procedures in dealing with learning problems). In the event that the student disagrees with the written evaluation statement prepared by the field instructor, he or she may include an addendum to the evaluation that states the student's interpretation of the facts. This should be encouraged and viewed as helpful to all concerned. Students should feel comfortable in signing their evaluations, which, in fact, become a contract between the student and agency for ongoing work at a particular level of learning and within a specified setting. Thus evaluations fulfill critical functions, including a review of student progress, or lack thereof, and a direction and emphasis for future learning. They also serve as the formal communication and accountability document between the agency and the school.[10]

SUMMARY

Selection of learning experiences for students in field practice requires extensive collaborative planning on the part of schools, agencies, field instructors, and students. Schools must be clear about the expectations for students and formulate guidelines that are applicable to a variety of field settings. Field settings must provide the necessary supports for students to learn about the system in which client needs are met, its place in the community, and ways in which new theoretical content can be connected to practice. Students must assume responsibility for their own learning and freely invest in the learning process.

Viewing the social work student as an adult learner is important in selecting the kinds, timing, and amount of experience. The tutorial approach used in field instruction allows the instructor to treat the student individually and to select the most appropriate experiences to meet the student's learning needs. Early learning experiences for undergraduate and first-level graduate students can include a study of their field-placement settings and the communities in which they are located as well as client–worker observational opportunities. Both students and field instructors should have guidelines and expectations, so they clearly understand the purposes and use of procedures.

Field instruction is an important educational experience through which students can be guided and supported in integrating theory with practice and in achieving a better balance among thinking, feeling, and doing. Through the process, self-awareness is stimulated and professional values are clarified and integrated. The evaluation process sums up achievements and identifies ongoing learning goals. It is also a valuable tool for the school in future planning and research purposes related to the field-instruction component of social work education.

REFERENCES

1. Francis Manis, *Openness in Social Work Field Instruction* (Goleta, Calif.: Kimberly Press, 1979), pp. 33–36.

2. Eleanor Hannon Judah, "Acculturation to the Social Work Profession in Baccalaureate Social Work Education," *Journal for Social Work* 12 (Fall

1976): 65–71; and Marion H. Wijnberg and Mary C. Schwartz, "Models of Student Supervision: The Apprentice, Growth, and Role Systems Models," *Journal of Education for Social Work* 13 (Fall 1977): 107–13.

3. Malcolm S. Knowles, *The Adult Learner: A Neglected Species* (Houston, Tex.: Gulf Publishing Company, 1973), pp. 77–79.

4. Hazel G. Price, "Achieving a Balance Between Self-Directed and Required Learning," *Journal of Education for Social Work* 12 (Winter 1976): 105–12.

5. Merle M. Foeckler and Gerald Boynton, "Creative Adult Learning-Teaching: Who's the Engineer of This Train?" *Journal of Education for Social Work* 12 (Fall 1976): 37–43.

6. Bernece K. Simon, "Design of Learning Experiences in Field Instruction," *The Social Service Review* 40 (December 1966): 397–409.

7. Max Siporin, "The Process of Field Instruction," *Quality Field Instruction in Social Work*, ed. Bradford W. Sheafor and Lowell E. Jenkins (New York: Longman, Inc., 1982), pp. 175–97.

8. Anne Minahan and Allen Pincus, "Conceptual Framework for Social Work Practice," *Social Work* 22 (September 1977): 347–52.

9. Teresa M. Schmidt, "The Development of Self-Awareness in First-Year Social Work Students," *Smith College Studies in Social Work* 46 (June 1976): 218–35.

10. Alex Gitterman and Naomi Pines Gitterman, "Social Work Student Evaluation: Format and Method," *Journal of Education for Social Work* 15 (Fall 1979): 103–108.

4

RECORDING

Student recording — the right kind of student recording — is capable of producing a foundation for the development of self-awareness.

— Francis Manis

Recording is used as a teaching tool in social work education. Although many schools stress the use of a particular style of recording for learning and teaching purposes, there is no standardized form. Consequently, the use of recording in education has little positive carry-over to its use in practice. Educators may ignore their responsibility with regard to this issue because a standardized form to which practice can relate does not exist. Rather, graduates are expected to adjust to the assorted styles of recording as they move from agency to agency. Thus the value of recording in practice is deemphasized rather than recognized as a useful tool for social workers.

Responsibility for formulating a streamlined design for recording that would elevate the social work record to a useful scientific document and stimulate the social worker toward professional self-development rests with both practitioners and educators. Practitioners can contribute to the elimination of ineffective record keeping by carefully scrutinizing the present system of recording and testing new approaches that would emphasize three essential qualities: (1) brevity in presentation, (2) concreteness in planning, and (3) evidence of intervention. Social work education can contribute to the solution by employing recording not only as a teaching tool but as a practical device graduates can use in their service to clients and in their own professional development.

Recording in education and practice has two principal purposes: (1) to provide a written account of progress and (2) to document the results of interventions. It should provide accountability to the profession and agency, to other professionals involved in the client's intervention, and to the client. In addition, recording provides an opportunity for self-development of the social worker in ongoing practice. Although both should be given equal weight, the focus in education is on self-development, whereas practice emphasizes service and accountability.

The present chapter examines ways in which recording can be used in education and practice so that it becomes useful for the social worker, the agency, and the profession, thus ultimately assuring the best service to clients. This chapter examines the purposes and objectives of recording in both social work education and practice and identifies progressive steps in the development of recording skills by the student, which, when accomplished, indicate readiness for the relevant use of recording in practice. Finally, the chapter focuses on significant ideas that emphasize the need for a unified format for recording practices.

RECORDING IN PRACTICE

Objectives

Before any substantive changes are made in our system of record keeping, we must understand the role that recording plays and its objectives. In practice, recording should (1) aid the worker in thinking through goals and direction, (2) provide evidence of progress with the client, (3) provide a measure of accountability for both the profession and the agency, and (4) assure the client of continuity of care.

Needs

Professional workers must emphasize the cognitive and intellectual aspects of practice and be open to rigorous analysis of their own work. Moreover, the profession needs common elements and consistency in recording for a common base in social work practice.[1] We can no longer afford the luxury of allowing a mystique to surround the social worker's role, the attitude that the social worker is an artist who is free to do his or her own thing, or the secrecy that goes under the guise and excuse of confidentiality. Social work practice needs a system of record keeping that provides for accountability.

Accountability. The demand for accountability in social work is similar to the energy crisis. The profession has been aware of the need to produce evidence of what it is doing, but it has taken a crisis to motivate the profession into doing something significant about it. Resources are available for solving the crisis, but they need to be explored and developed. Exploration takes time and effort. The crisis of accountability in the social work profession highlights the need for a system of accountability that focuses on results as well as process. Among other deficiencies, case studies and case histories do not show controlled conditions, the influence of the intervention, the relative overall number of successes and failures, and the long-term effects and cost.[2] It is interesting that presentations of case histories are one of the few consistencies in professional recording. Accountability has many facets, recording being only one. Accountability can be established by statistical or research data stored in the computer or in terms of dollars and cents. A unified recording system, however, makes a valuable contribution to alleviating the crisis of accountability.

Record keeping. It is impossible to perform an empirical evaluation of effort without adequate records. The records of human service agencies are often in abysmal condition.[3] This is an unnecessary state of affairs. Recording can include many measurable aspects, for example, a high correlation of certain problems that occur concurrently and sequentially, a connection between the results of the treatment and the therapeutic techniques used by the social worker and time involved, and kinds and uses of environmental resources that facilitated or hampered treatment.

Problems for Practice

Recording as a process is used by educational institutions for teaching and learning purposes and frequently does not move beyond this stage in social work education. There is little discussion of recording outside the field-practice courses. Moreover, recording is so inconsistently used in field-practice courses that it cannot help but become an obstacle to the professional social worker, as exemplified in the following statement: "Although few caseworkers enjoy recording, it seems that the deeply ingrained injunction, thou shalt record in detail, was very much a part of their professional self-concept."[4] Recording is used to help social work students think in an organized and disciplined way but is not always used to help practicing social workers expand and develop their thinking. The reason for this is that recording as a technique has not been sharpened, updated, or changed with the growth of the profession. Consequently, it has fallen into obsolescence and even disrepute among many practitioners.

Progress in the Use of Recording for Social Work Practice

Noel Timms presented a thorough review of the literature on recording in social work to 1972. He noted that the last text that had been published on the topic was one by Gordon Hamilton in 1946 and that most of the articles in the literature deal with particular aspects of recording.[5] More recently, Suanna Wilson responded to this lack of information in her book on recording.[6] She offers suggestions to field instructors in evaluating student recording and discusses the differences between beginning and more advanced interviews. In addition, the book provides concrete approaches to and examples of other types of recording necessary for student learning.

A review of research on the outcomes of social work intervention indicates that although results on the effectiveness of social work therapeutic intervention were uncertain, they appear to point in a negative direction. It was suggested that much more work is needed to delineate the specific characteristics of the body of techniques we call psychotherapy. After these techniques have been delineated, they must be evaluated on the basis of desired outcome for given populations.[7] Unless social workers understand their techniques and goals in working with clients, no style of recording will help. Because research is somewhat dependent on the case record for information, the profession will be caught in a vicious circle until steps are taken to clarify intervention techniques and goals.

Suggestions for revising case-recording methods have ranged from recording by code to recording at the beginning and the end of the client contacts. Although all suggested methods have potential in that they save time and value uniformity, information is lacking on the progression of results in many of the methods.

A system of recording by code was set up in the 1960s in an attempt to evaluate the effectiveness of social work with acting-out youth.[8] This approach to recording was undertaken by the Seattle Atlantic Street Center of Seattle, Washington, because of the problems the then current method posed for evaluative research, the need to standardize recording procedure, and a desire to contribute to the knowledge base of social work practice. The evaluation of the instrument — which was designed to incorporate the total activity of a social worker operating from a multiple-methodological base as he or she interacted with expansive client systems — indicated possible uses of the method and clarified the areas that needed to be adjusted.[9] The method particularly helped workers sharpen their practice and research skills. Considerable effort went into identifying the techniques and activity of the worker, and the method appeared to have potential for further refinement.

A workshop cosponsored by the Midwest Region and the National Services of the Jewish Welfare Board also was initiated to develop a standard of measurement for evaluating service to clients.

These groups were concerned that social workers usually depended on describing rather than evaluating their programs. Often unconsciously, social workers avoided any attempt to measure whether the outcomes were coextensive with the high-sounding promises of the program.[10] The workshop produced some indicators in behavioral terms that would objectively evaluate results and measure progress against the originally stated objectives or purpose. To what extent the findings of this workshop were put into operation is not known, but the results that evolved have potential for development and are at least a step in the right direction.

RECORDING IN EDUCATION

Process recording should be used during students' initial stage of learning, during beginning contacts with new clients, and when students are experiencing problems. It should not be the only means of recording throughout their education, and it should not be used in professional practice other than for training purposes. Unless students learn to develop their use of recording throughout their academic program, the recording tool will lose both its usefulness and value. It is important, therefore, to adjust the style of recording to meet the needs of students in their particular stage of learning so that they reach a level of skill in writing that is useful in practice and produces the qualities of brevity, concreteness, and evidence of intervention.

In general, there are three stages of recording for learners: (1) process, (2) combining two or more interviews, and (3) orientation for practice.

Process Recording

Process recording should have two general objectives:

1. To help students develop awareness of the client's behavior, responses, and surroundings, and self-awareness in how they relate to the client
2. To establish a framework for the development of an organized, disciplined approach to the problem-solving process

Students usually understand the value of developing an overall awareness of an interview through their recordings. They are less clear about the second objective and may need some form of structure or explicit guidance. It is important that field instructors not only provide this structure for students but also help them use the structure to achieve the objectives. When first using recording, students direct much of their energy toward remembering the events and observations within the interview. Responses from a group of students who were requested to indicate their learning gains from using process recording consistently fell into two areas: "It forces you to go over what transpired; it represents a tangible and helpful method of remembering what a client said and the need to connect it with how he felt at the time." "It prepares you to think about and write a biopsychosocial assessment, but after a while you begin to write the recordings without much thought."[11] (See Appendix A for sample process recording and discussion.) After students develop their capacity to recall the events of the interview and their awareness of both the clients' responses and their own, they are ready to move toward new objectives, which require an adjustment in the recording tool.

Combining Interviews

By the beginning of the second semester, most undergraduate and first-level graduate students need to take a fresh look at process recording. At this point there are three objectives for the use of recording:

Ability to connect interviews. Students are often vague as to why they are seeing the client. They may not give serious thought to the purpose of the interview until it is time to do the recording. This fact becomes particularly evident when students can no longer rely on providing tangible services or when they must come to grips with "doing for" the client. At this stage in their development, students are able to verbalize the importance of making a connection between tangible services as a means for identifying other difficulties or concerns. Students generally recognize the need to be better prepared for interviews and begin to prepare themselves, but they frequently neglect to make the connection between the content of the interview and the plan for their next contact.

Motivating clients to understand, make conclusions about, or resolve their concerns. Although students have developed an awareness of themselves in the helping process, they are not necessarily conscious of conclusions that are reached by clients or of the steps involved in assisting the clients to achieve their goals. Progress is not easily achieved and may even be difficult to identify. Facts of the case may be discouraging and disappointing for students unless they know what to look for, when to move to a deeper level of intervention, and how to measure progress or regression on the part of the client. At this point, students and field instructors are able to evaluate students' capacity to respond to and deal with the clients' feelings and concerns and are able to clarify mutually the required learning needs for developing their ability to help.

Preparing clients for ongoing contacts. Consciously involving the client in ongoing contacts is another objective that is difficult to attain. Students require considerable help in connecting their goals with those of the client. Frequently, they tell the client the plan for the next interview or to set up an appointment simply assuming that the client knows the purpose of the next interview. This approach usually results from students' eagerness to achieve stated goals and relates to where students are in the learning process, rather than where clients are in terms of their capacity to receive and use help. Students often feel that their initial description of themselves and their eagerness to help are sufficient to carry them through the remainder of their contacts with clients. Consequently, they need to become more aware of the importance of ongoing clarification of their role with the client. Learning how to terminate the interview and how to involve the client in preparing for the following interview is helpful, particularly for students who need to change or expand the concept of their role.

Orientation for Professional Practice

After students develop a conscious awareness of how to use themselves more appropriately, an appreciation of the need for a disciplined approach to problem solving, and the capacity to identify movement on the part of the clients, they can begin to think about shifting their style of recording. The record should be concise and pinpoint clients' concerns, resolutions, and how these resolutions were achieved. The objectives at this point should stress the following:

1. The continued development of students' own professional skill but with a stronger emphasis on the agency's concern for effective services to clients (shift from self-focus to client and service)

2. The ability to translate their knowledge and skill into a written record that is brief and concrete and that identifies the results of their contacts with clients

If students have learned and experienced the need to clarify their goals with the client, can recognize the value of being prepared for interviews, and are consciously aware of using themselves, they will welcome and be challenged by a new style of recording. It will continue to stimulate them to think while making them responsible for providing information about what they are doing without detail and description. (See Appendix A for sample recording.)

OTHER MODELS OF RECORDING

The medical profession has raised similar concerns about its record-keeping system, which, many feel, has resulted in inefficiency in education and practice and in the absence of a system of meaningful audit in the practice of medicine. Lawrence L. Weed presented the medical profession with a record-keeping method that was designed to continually remind physicians to think systematically about their patients and to provide evidence of whether they have actually done so.[12] The Weed method recognizes four basic elements: (1) establishment of a data base, (2) formulation of all problems (problem list), (3) plans for treatment of each problem, and (4) follow-up on each problem. These areas are delineated so that all aspects are covered in a complete, concise manner. The first three elements are comparable to the biopsychosocial assessment in social work practice. Weed's follow-up phase of record keeping (or progress notes) includes subjective data, objective data, interpretation, and immediate plans. He stresses the importance of teaching physicians in training to properly organize progress notes during their early education of the physician in order to create a framework upon which to build the students' postgraduate self-education.

A problem-oriented recording model for social work settings was developed based on the Weed method.[13] This model provides a systematized approach to diagnosis and treatment and facilitates teaching, research, and monitoring for quality control of practice. Many social work settings have made adjustments in their recording system based on this model and find that it improves their record keeping. A problem-oriented log (POL) for improving casework accountability has been identified and described by George Burrill. He believes that the clarity and focus of this model allow the worker a wider scope for creative solution of specific problems.[14]

SUMMARY

The resistance of social work practice to the scientific method is reflected in the profession's reluctance to document and produce evidence of its methods and results. Both practice and education must deal with this concern; the system of recording is a good place to begin. In social work education, recording is used as an effective teaching tool, but little effort has been made to use recording in practice apart from its application in teaching and learning.

In many ways the carry-over has been negative — one that suggests detail or avoidance. In teaching, as in practice, recording requires standardization. Furthermore, instructors should introduce a sequence of styles that will coordinate with the students' overall progress in learning. How recording is used in teaching relates directly to what students are expected to achieve; these expectations should be understood by field instructors and students. Students need structure and guidelines to help them reach their goals. Well-thought-through approaches to recording can provide both. After teaching students to use recording to achieve the early phase of self-focus, the field instructor should help students to use recording to think more clearly about the relatedness of client contacts and the responses of the client to help. If this is done, students will begin to achieve a more conscious, disciplined use of self. Moreover, they will begin to see the correlation among problems and take responsibility for follow-up on the identified concerns of the client.

Field instructors need clear evidence of the level of the student's performance. Recording can provide this evidence. In addition, recording can help field instructors identify students' learning patterns and ascertain in what learning areas students need further help.

In practice, recording must be explored further. The record should be a document that emphasizes effectiveness, facilitates research, and aids in monitoring for quality control. As Weed states,

> Failure to keep accurate and up-to-date records may be regarded as a form of secrecy. When a physician restricts the knowledge of his art to himself by keeping unintelligible records, he may be denying his patient the illumination that is his right. Indian medicine men and ancient Egyptian priests guarded their secrets to keep uninformed and fearful patients in their grip. That failure to create the kind of medical record that will tell everyone authorized to know exactly what a physician has done is an analogous form of secrecy — and secrecy has no place in the science of medical practice.[15]

This statement is timely and appropriate for the social work profession as well.

REFERENCES

1. Harriet M. Bartlett, *The Common Base in Social Work Practice* (New York: National Association of Social Workers, 1970), p. 40.

2. Edward Newman and Jerry Turem, "The Crisis of Accountability," *Social Work* 19 (January 1974): 5–16.

3. Emil Posavac and Raymond C. Carey, *Program Evaluation: Method and Case Studies* (Englewood Cliffs, N.J.: Prentice Hall, 1980).

4. Sarah T. Lusby and Bernice D. Rudney, "One Agency's Solution to the Recording Problem," *Social Casework* 54 (December 1973): 588.

5. Noel Timms, *Recording in Social Work* (London and Boston: Routledge and Kegan Paul, 1972).

6. Suanna J. Wilson, *Recording: Guidelines for Social Workers* (New York: Free Press, 1980).

7. Steven P. Segal, "Research on the Outcome of Social Work Therapeutic Intervention: A Review of Literature," *Journal of Health and Social Behavior* 13 (March 1972): 3–17.

8. James R. Seaberg, "Case Recording by Code," *Social Work* 10 (October 1965): 92–98.

9. James R. Seaberg, "Systematized Recording: A Follow-up," *Social Work* 15 (October 1970): 32–41.

10. Joseph Soffen, ed., "A Guide for Creating Tools for Program Evaluation," in *Proceedings of Training Institute for Jewish Center Workers* (Chicago, Ill.: Chicago National Jewish Welfare Board, March 1968), p. 1.

11. Martha Urbanowski, "Recording to Measure Effectiveness," *Social Casework* 55 (November 1974): 546–53.

12. Lawrence L. Weed, *Medical Records, Medical Education and Patient Care* (Cleveland, Ohio: The Press of Case Western Reverve, 1971).

13. Wilma M. Martens and Elizabeth Holmstrum, "Problem-Oriented Recording," *Social Casework* 55 (November 1974): 554–61.

14. George C. Burrill, "The Problem-Oriented Log in Social Casework," *Social Work* 21 (January 1976): 67–68.

15. Weed, *Medical Records, Medical Education and Patient Care*, p. 124.

5

PROCESS RECORDING

Process recording can be an effective way of monitoring student interviews and also a dynamic teaching tool.

—*Suanna J. Wilson*

Substantial gains have been made in refining the methods of social work education, although process recording — one of the most central elements in students' field instruction — remains virtually unchanged. However, a more structured kind of process recording should be taught by field instructors, one that is more educationally sound and ultimately less time consuming for students. Intellectual clarity and logical structure, both of which are essential in classroom teaching and learning, should be accorded the same importance in field instruction; they are particularly appropriate in student process recording.

WHAT IS PROCESS RECORDING?

Is it possible for social work educators to agree on the meaning of the term process recording as used in field instruction, or is the term vague, undefined, and subject to widely different interpretations? There is at least general agreement that process recording is the written account of the dynamic interaction that occurs during an interview or in other forms of client contact. This written account contains factual information, the student's responses to the concerns and behavior of those involved in the contact, and the activities that attempt to resolve the client's concerns. Furthermore, process recording encompasses a detailed analysis of the student's observations of and reactions to the client contact.[1] Thus the student's earliest training in recording gives special emphasis to reporting a wealth of detail and places relatively little emphasis on the structure of the written account. Although it is essential that students learn to recall detail, structure is also an important quality in process recordings and will in fact help students identify essential details and stimulate recall of the major interactions with clients.

VALUE OF PROCESS RECORDING

It would be difficult to devise a satisfactory substitute for process recording for beginning undergraduate and graduate students. Although it is time-consuming, frustrating, and difficult for both students and field instructors, it enhances students' professional learning and growth and is a valuable teaching tool for field instructors. The following highlights some of the values for both.

For the Student
- Serves as a basic instrument in guiding learning and helps the student conceptualize and organize ongoing activities with client systems
- Helps clarify the purpose of an interview or activity and the student's role in it
- Helps student rethink each client contact while realizing that the experience and interactions he or she has had with the client must be clearly communicated to the field instructor who reads the recordings
- Provides a basic tool for stimulating communication and self-awareness
- Furnishes the opportunity to acquire a measure of facility and freedom in written expression, both of which are important for professional development
- Permits both instructor and student to identify the student's strengths and weaknesses without the student feeling threatened or exposed
- Provides a base for developing summarized and other styles of recording required by the agency and educational institution

For the Field Instructor
- Plays an important part in providing direction and structural framework for the field-instruction conference
- Provides opportunity to treat individually both students and clients with whom students are working
- Enables the field instructor to assess quickly the student's ability to respond to the feeling content of interviews or activities with clients
- Reflects the extent to which students are able to integrate knowl-

edge and theory gained from previous experiences, classroom courses, and outside readings
- Assists in planning for evaluation conferences

The extent to which recording becomes a vehicle for students' continued growth or a roadblock to their advancement depends on how it is used as a teaching device. Guidelines on the respective responsibilities for using process recording should be established for both students and field instructors. If field instructors do not provide meaningful feedback, the purpose of the process recording is negated; and if students are not open and honest in their process recording, they cheat themselves.[2]

PROBLEMS

In Learning

The learning process has been described as having five stages that each learner must complete, regardless of individual characteristics or level of skill: (1) beginning or orientation, (2) defining the learning problem, (3) struggling with the learning problem in the supervisor–worker relationship, (4) making a breakthrough to independent functioning, and (5) evaluating the learning process itself.[3] Although unstructured process recording can be useful, especially in the first stage of the learning process, it gradually diminishes in value throughout the other four stages. Field instructors cannot use it as a means to identify students' learning patterns or as an aid in the formulation of educational goals. Furthermore, unstructured process recording does not help students develop their ability to see cause-and-effect relationships, identify pertinent information, or conceptualize information.

In Teaching

As in classroom courses, the content of field instruction must be identified and plainly communicated to students. Field instruction should help students approach problem solving in an orderly, disciplined manner, so they can build on the experience they bring to field practice while integrating new knowledge. Coverage of content, however, poses special problems for field instructors in that knowledge must be taught according to the needs of the client and the function of the agency rather than in the systematic manner used in the classroom. Field instructors largely depend, therefore, on the content of the students' recordings in teaching the elements of social work practice. Without some structure to this teaching and learning instrument, students may feel lost in the maze of content that is covered.

In Professional Practice

Discursive, extremely detailed recording does not in itself equip students to meet the professional demands that are made of them later. Because students invest so much of their field-practice time in recording, one would expect that by the end of their field experience they would be able to formulate their thoughts clearly in writing in keeping with the expectations of the undergraduate or graduate levels of professional education. When they become agency staff members, recording continues to consume a disproportionate amount of their time and is often postponed until it reaches unmanageable proportions. A variety of new styles of recording are being introduced in social agencies, most of which are highly structured and require workers to be specific and think analytically. Case records must provide documentation of the goals achieved in the intervention process and how these were accomplished. New graduates are often unable to make the transition from the method of recording required by the educational process to the type of process recording that they are expected to produce as professional social workers.

Why Structure Is Necessary

How can process recording be retained as a valuable tool for learning without becoming a handicap? The answer lies in introducing structure in student recording. Students often ask for structure; it can be beneficial in the learning process. Field instructors may fear that if students are expected to structure their recordings, interviews with clients may become too highly structured and result in a rigid, stereotyped client–worker interaction and constriction in the use of self. Actually, the opposite is true. Structured recording can help students appreciate the value of process recording and use it more effectively. It helps clarify their thinking about the purpose of an interview or client contact and their role in the relationship. It serves as a basic guide in their learning and helps them to apply concepts learned in classes and organize their ongoing client activities. It directs students toward a conscious awareness of the interaction between themselves and their clients and the skills that are used and eventually allows them to identify the factors that effect change and create stability in clients.

Emphasizing structure in recording does not hamper the students' creativity and freedom to be themselves in interactions with their clients. Rather, it helps students to assume greater responsibility for their own learning. The field instructor is obligated to create an educational climate in which students feel comfortable with recording and develop a positive attitude toward it as a learning device and a professional skill.

APPROACH TO STRUCTURED RECORDING

Beginning students must be provided with an operational framework that can be adapted to their particular needs, educational level, and rate of growth and development. The following outline of recording content is offered as a guide to students and field instructors. It provides sufficient structure for students to begin thinking in a disciplined and organized manner while allowing them to exercise freedom of choice and creativity.

Purpose of Client Contact

Students should be asked to formulate a statement of purpose that is concise, clear, and specific in relation to the proposed interview or encounter with the client. It should show the relation between the current meeting and the previous contact and should reflect the student's awareness of the particular function of the agency and of the client's capacity and motivation.

Observations

This section of the recording varies in length and content in accordance with the stage of the student–client relationship. More detail is likely to be needed during the initial contacts. Students should record general impressions of the physical and emotional climate at the outset of meeting and its specific impact on the client. Significant changes in the client's appearance or surroundings are also important.

Content

This part of the recording should describe the interaction between the client and student during the planned contact. Although each student develops his or her own style of writing, this section should include the following:

1. Description of how the interview or activity began
2. Pertinent information discussed with the client and responses of both client and student in relation to it
3. Description of the interaction between the client and student in dealing with the purpose and the concerns identified during the

client contact, including facts and feelings revealed by both client and student

4. Description of the client's preparation for the next interview or activity and a statement of how the contact ended

Impressions

As early as students' first contact with their clients, students should state their impressions based on the facts. This process gradually develops into analytical thinking as students integrate course content and gain understanding of the interaction between themselves and their clients.

Worker's Role

This section should highlight the students' activity with clients and reflect use of social work roles, skills, and techniques. Students should evaluate their effectiveness as helping persons in each interview or encounter with the client.

Plan

Students should briefly state plans for the next contact and record thoughts about long-range goals for their clients.[4]

USE OF RECORDING IN TEACHING/LEARNING

Timing

Students' ability to expose themselves to risk in recording is largely dependent on their relationship with their field instructors. Students differ in regard to when they are ready to become selective in their recording of the "content" of the interview. Since students are unique in terms of life experience, previous acquaintance with social work, personal talents, and cultural backgrounds, field instructors must tailor their use of recording to students' individual needs.

Selectivity

Undergraduates and first-level graduate students become more selective during the second semester of field practice and begin to record in three or four pages what previously required five or six pages. Greater selectivity in recording the content of the interview has a twofold result: (1) it makes thinking more concise and disciplined, and (2) it consumes less time. Students should continue to record material on the purpose of the interview and their impressions, role, and plan. They may need to record their observations and detailed content only for the first few interviews or contacts with a new client or when special problems or significant changes occur for either themselves or their client. This approach to recording enhances students' later adjustment to the professional demands of an agency and enables them to see recording in its true perspective, that is, as an aid to practice rather than as a burden. (See Appendix A for a sample process recording and discussion.)

SUMMARY

If one accepts the premise that the primary role of the field instructor is to educate, then it follows that a certain amount of structure in the education is essential. Developing a format for process recording is a beginning. Structured process recording can be a valuable teaching/learning tool in the field-instruction component of social work education.

Process recording provides students with a framework for thinking in an organized and disciplined way. It stimulates students to become actively involved in learning through assessment of their client contacts. Students better understand the various roles of the social worker and how they can use themselves in these roles. A structured format for process recording can help students develop their conceptual ability and improve writing skills.

For field instructors process recording helps individualize students and provides direction in teaching. It enables field instructors to plan more effectively for the educational needs of their students and to determine the gaps in learning. It is invaluable for pulling together students' progress over a period of time and in adding a measure of objectivity to evaluations.

REFERENCES

1. Margaret Dwyer and Martha Urbanowski, "Student Process Recording: A Plea for Structure," *Social Casework* 46 (May 1965): 283–86.

2. Suanna J. Wilson, *Recording: Guidelines for Social Workers* (New York: Free Press, 1980), pp. 23–25.

3. Fred Berl, "The Content and Method of Supervisory Teaching," *Social Casework* 44 (November 1963): 516–22.

4. Dwyer and Urbanowski, "Student Process Recording," pp. 285–86.

6

LEARNING PATTERNS IN FIELD PRACTICE

The educator does not attempt to know the basic cause of the anxiety. He does attempt to know the precipitants in the educational situation.

— Charlotte Towle

Understanding adult learners requires social work educators to think about, identify, and evaluate ways in which students learn. Not much emphasis has been given to this facet of teaching, possibly because of the concern about coverage of content and meeting the expectations of performance. Both coverage of content and meeting expectations of performance are important; both can be achieved more effectively if the instructor understands and appreciates the ways in which social work students learn. This seems to be especially pertinent for learning in field practice.

The present chapter reviews studies and theories on the ways students learn that have been presented in social work literature. Learning patterns of students and ways in which field instructors can use the individual student's style of learning in mastering content and achieving performance goals are identified. In addition, the need for students to think about and identify their own learning patterns is discussed.

STUDIES ON LEARNING PATTERNS

Several important contributions have been made in an attempt to identify styles or patterns of learning of social work students. As early as 1955, a study of graduate students was conducted to determine the pattern or patterns of learning in individual students and whether such patterns could be grouped into clusters.[1] The results identified three subpatterns that characterized the most prominent aspects of the ways students learned: the experiential-empathic learner, the doer, and the intellectual-empathic learner. The behaviors of each of these types of learners were examined in seven major areas: students' selective responses to learning demands; responsibility and use of supervision in learning; timing, quality, and handling of anxiety; quality of conceptualization and use of previous experience; stimuli associated with positive learning responses; time pattern; and performance qualities.

A study of how social work practitioners relate to abstract knowledge described two models of orientation to knowledge: (1) the active, open-system learner who actively seeks out and welcomes new knowledge and (2) the passive, closed-system learner who wards off new knowledge and tends usually to reject new and unfamiliar concepts.[2] Both models assume that the learner has a normal capacity for cognitive as well as intuitive forms of learning. The usefulness of these models was tested in order to identify and distinguish casework practitioners' dominant stances in regard to abstract knowledge. The association between orientation to knowledge and learning from practice experience was also studied. Results indicated a significantly high correlation between orientation to abstract knowledge and the capacity to learn conceptually from practice. Open-system learners consistently outperformed closed-system learners on every task. It is clear from the results of this study that practitioners differ in orientation to knowledge in systematically patterned ways that are subject to study.

Patterns of responses to the stimulation of new knowledge are described in various studies. These include (1) learners who can make very pertinent and shrewd theoretical social diagnoses but who find it very difficult to apply their skill to helping the client, (2) learners who want to apply knowledge immediately to practice but the excitement of learning limits their capacity for observation in practice, and (3) learners who respond to new learning with caution and continue using old ways of responding to clients.[3] Differing behaviors can be identified between students who feel threatened before they have the theoretical framework and students who have a natural "feel" for people and intuitively pick up and use what clients are trying to communicate.

An empirical study identified differing styles of learning in social work students who were preparing for direct social work practice.[4] In this study three modes of cognitive activity were selected:

1. *Conceptual (objective, theoretical):* dimension of functioning through which the student develops a core of knowledge about and for practice.

2. *Affective (subjective, value-based):* dimension of functioning through which the student develops awareness of emotions, atti-

tudes, and motivational factors in the self and others in the social work situation.

3. *Operational (active):* dimension of functioning through which the student achieves skill in utilizing the knowledge base in relationships bounded by professional purpose.

An instrument that described the three hypothetical models of learners for direct practice was devised; students arranged these models into a pattern that reflected their own learning style. Instructors — both classroom and field — also rated students' performance in the learner role.

The results indicated that social work students preferred the operational (active) mode and believed it to be the mode by which they learned the best. Both affective and operational modes were rated above the conceptual mode. The academic and field instructors rated the students in a similar manner and evaluated the learners who responded conceptually as being more successful students. The self-profiling of learning styles was useful to both students and field instructors. Field instructors were better able to individualize the learners, and students gained new insight and self-awareness of a dimension of their functioning that had not been stressed before.

Gerald M. Gross uses the term "learner characteristics" to denote relatively stable, educationally relevant, individual differences in students. He discusses four orientations of learners, which were identified and elaborated on by David Hunt:[5]

1. *Cognitive orientation:* requiring a degree of structure in the learning environment

2. *Motivational orientation:* requiring a form of feedback and reward

3. *Value orientation:* requiring value context of the instructional presentation

4. *Sensory orientation:* requiring modality of media and size of presentation.

Gross addresses the need for instructional design efforts and proposes a theoretical framework to guide instructional design of strategies in social work education. He makes a good case for the need to understand and blend the conceptual, affective, and operational learning modes in the field-instruction component of social work education.

LEARNING PATTERNS IN FIELD PRACTICE

Each student has a unique way of learning. Nevertheless, from a review of the studies that have been done, from other descriptive material in the literature, and from our own observations as field instructors, some learning patterns seem to be common to all students in field practice. Identifying and clarifying these common patterns is helpful from the teaching perspective because it enables field instructors to better understand what it means to "individualize the learner." In addition, it provides direction for implementing a tailor-made teaching approach and makes it easier to relate to and teach a variety of learners.

Patterns of Learning

Obviously, no person fits a learning pattern in all its details. Nonetheless, each person has some identifiable characteristics. The following defines three patterns of learning.

1. *Intellectual (thinking):* Students' initial approach and means of effecting change are through the intellect. Students are able to identify problems more clearly by analysis. In formulating hypotheses, students draw upon generalizations that they already know and have used to solve problems without going through many of the normal steps of the problem-solving process.

2. *Intuitive (feeling):* The initial approach and means of effecting change are through the use of natural skills in working with people. The students are not consciously aware of their responses or capabilities, only that they gain considerable satisfaction in their direct contacts with clients. Students tend to rely on instinctive knowledge and feelings to carry them through.

3. *Experiential (doing):* The initial approach and means of effecting change are gained by practice, trial, and observation. Students are able to see what is happening from their performance; from their experience, they are able to incorporate intellectual content. It is easier for these students to move from the specific to the general.

Intellectual Learner

Behavioral characteristics. At the beginning of the field-placement experience, intellectual learners tend to assume a great deal of initiative in learning. The students feel secure because they have read widely, analyzed their situation, and developed a frame of reference within which they relate to social work professionals and clients. The students are stimulated by the theoretical content of academic courses and are successful in this area. Their early case recordings reflect interest in people, freedom to speculate about the meaning of behavior, and a capacity to identify both tangible problems and problems that deal with feelings.

As the field experience progresses, these students demonstrate a special skill in the diagnostic area. They are organized, logical, concise, and able to conceptualize. However, difficulties may arise when they must do more than provide tangible services. Since theoretical learning is so effortless for them, these students become frustrated with the need to think through the interactions involved in the relationship process. Their levels of self-expectation are high, and they become easily discouraged by their lack of success in "doing."

In their early contacts with the client, they are able to identify obstacles. It is difficult, however, to move these students from problem focus to client focus. They are overly prepared for interviews and are frustrated when flexibility is required. As a result they sometimes fail to grasp the importance of working at the pace of the client. The students' need to effect change quickly may overwhelm the client and result in termination or lack of any significant response.

Intellectual learners experience problems with field learning and place many demands on field instructors. Many of their problems stem from their strong desire to succeed and their fear of being forced to act before they have sufficient knowledge based on course content. Consequently, when they are forced to focus on the emotional content of the helping relationship, their security is threatened. The students react to this insecurity by seeking a magic formula that provides clear and explicit instructions on how to help clients beyond tangible needs. They are threatened by criticism and less free to expose themselves to risk. They protect themselves by attempting to control conference periods. They may focus on details about which they are knowledgeable or attempt to engage in abstract reasoning.

Making changes in their manner of relating to clients is difficult for these learners; frequently, they can adapt superficially without really changing. Self-awareness, consequently, is much more painful for these students. They struggle hard and long to hold onto old patterns of learning and performing, frequently fearing that they will lose status in the intellectual area and will regress rather than develop.

Teaching approach. Intellectual learners are not as easily identified as are the other two types of learners. Intellectual learners tend to protect themselves with their ability to achieve and produce on an intellectual level. Learning may proceed at an intellectual level but break down when put to practical use. Although intellectual grasp is a first step from the standpoint of the aims of professional education, the student has not changed until he or she can *do* differently.[6] These students take the first step in their education smoothly and successfully; field instructors must help them take the next step by helping them experience some success in practice beyond the giving of tangible services or implementing agency procedures.

Intellectual learners need time to examine how theory applies to a particular situation before being able to integrate one with the other. Caution should be taken not to force them into the feeling areas before they are ready. As this process continues, field instructors need to constantly stimulate discussions of feeling areas on the part of clients and students. Frequently, the students are cognizant of meaningful responses from clients but require help with their own responses. Additional efforts should focus on helping intellectual learners perceive various elements of a situation so as to stimulate their curiosity and imagination.

Selecting a variety of case material helps intellectual learners redirect their tendency to categorize people. Learning needs, in general, are most effectively met by increased emphasis on case assignments and, subsequently, more contact with clients. This helps students individualize clients and see their tendency to impose their own values on clients; it helps them to question causative factors for behavior early in the field experience. The variety and increased number of contacts also helps reorient students from focusing on the client's problems to focusing on the client with the problem.

Discussion of the social worker's role helps students recognize their own lack of emotional involvement and begin thinking about why their responses are not effective. This, in turn, leads them to look for alternative approaches and responses. It must be remembered, however, that intellectual learners are less introspective; consequently, their ability to understand their interactions with the client is internalized at a slower rate. Repetitious discussions may stimulate awareness of their interactions with clients, disciplined use of self in the interview, and the importance of their own feelings.

The students' freedom to admit their inadequacies is directly related to how comfortable they feel within their relationship with the field instructor. Students look to the field instructor as a model of the social work professional and often feel they must test the relationship before committing themselves to it. Instructors must be alert to their own feelings because of the provocative nature of intellectual learners' responses to supervision and the danger of perpetuating their inadequacies. Field instructors must be intellectually stimulating in order to help students recognize and work advantageously within their learning patterns, while stressing the strengths of the experiential and intuitive learning modes.

It takes time for these students to test, trust, and become comfortable with their feelings. Instructors may tend to react defensively to this type of learner, who may be perceived as a "know-it-all." It takes patience, effort, and time for field instructors to evaluate their own feelings toward these students and to arrive at teaching goals with the students.

Intuitive Learner

Behavioral characteristics. Intuitive learners meet with few major problems at the beginning of their placement. They are practical, extremely sensitive, and have a high degree of natural talent and established security in relating to people. Basically giving persons, they are enthusiastic about beginning with their cases and keenly motivated to understand how the agency can be utilized for the benefit of clients. Utilizing tangible services reinforces feelings of adequacy and encourages them to exhibit more initiative in discovering additional resources. They work steadily and diligently and assume considerable responsibility for managing their work load. At times, especially early in placement, they move ahead too quickly and fail to realize the need to explore existing agency policies and procedures. This failure is not usually based on an undue amount of conflict with authority but rather on their desire to follow their feeling instincts.

Intuitive learners tend to avoid an analytical, orderly approach to problem solving and spend a disproportionate amount of time on field-practice activities, often to the detriment of classroom demands for acquiring a broad base of theoretical knowledge. Early in their field-placement experience, they are quite enthusiastic about social work theory because they find it so compatible with their natural way of responding to others. Content from "Human Behavior in the Social Environment" and other theoretical courses is viewed as interesting but not especially useful except for its contribution to their general fund of knowledge. Because these students are so actively involved with the current functioning of clients, they question the emphasis on acquiring knowledge and understanding the dynamics of behavior. When intuitive learners begin to appreciate the benefits of an orderly, structured approach to problem solving, they begin to integrate theoretical content, improve their conceptual ability, and consciously use self in the helping process.

Early recordings reveal special skills in individualizing clients, recognizing strengths, and, to a lesser degree, weaknesses. Intuitive learners are able to identify client needs and focus on practical problems. They pay less attention to viewing the entire case situation. Their feeling responses toward clients are easily available to them, readily heard, and usually appropriate. As greater conceptualization is demanded from them, their style becomes more stilted and recordings briefer. During this period the students are especially resistant to integrating and using new knowledge. Although anxiety increases during this period, students are pushed toward self-examination in the helping process.

Initially, field instructors are quite impressed with the intuitive learner's ability to verbalize his or her identification with the social work profession. These students are amazed that they have found a profession in which they feel so comfortable, curious, and eager to learn. They feel free to question and are eager to engage the instructor in interesting discussions about the social work profession. However, when discussions are limited to helping students see concepts and understand principles in social work, intuitive learners often resist. They know they are successful with clients and initially feel defensive and fearful that they will lose their intuitive skill in helping people. Rather than becoming dependent on field instruction, they go through a phase in which they operate quite independently and often experience difficulty turning recordings in on time. This behavior continues until they gain confidence in themselves as learners. After they realize that integrating theoretical content with practical experience is not a major problem, they begin asking for and using instructional help.

Teaching approach. A teaching plan for intuitive learners should contain two key elements: (1) helping the students to conceptualize and (2) providing them with a clearly defined structure with which they can meet the intellectual demands. For all students, the ability to think conceptually is connected with their understanding of underlying theory. Intuitive learners must be stimulated to relate their skill in developing relationships to a more scientific and theoretical framework. They should be encouraged to relate their assessments and intervention plans in a particular case assignment to the general theoretical principles that are involved. Recognizing similarities as well as differences in their cases also facilitates changes in thinking and doing.

Early in the placement, intuitive learners need to become consciously aware of their strengths and to have these strengths reinforced. This awareness is essential if they are to understand their positive characteristics so they can change their negative characteristics. Improvement in handling cases can be achieved by limiting the number of cases assigned and curtailing undisciplined case activity, unlike the experiential or intellectual learner who requires a variety of case experiences. Selection of cases requires special consideration. Usually, these students work quite effectively with hostile, deprived, or acting-out clients. These clients are viewed as a challenge. Although they need to experience success from such cases, their integrative capacity can be facilitated through the assignment of other case situations. Nonverbal clients stimulate questions regarding the conscious use of self as well as more reflective thinking about cause-and-effect relationships.

The early inclusion of the social worker's role in recordings also helps develop the intuitive learner's integrative capacity by developing operational self-awareness. Summarization recording of several interviews often helps these students see a pattern of behavior. Focusing on the social worker's role, impressions, and planning also improves conceptualization. Without this emphasis, the written material remains essentially descriptive; although often accurate and lengthy, the material lacks succinctness and professionalism.

Intuitive learners need time, patience, and instructional help before they can be expected to integrate theory adequately and consistently. Field instructors should be prepared for the slumps that will occur, usually in proportion to the demands for depth in their assessments and interventions. Field instructors must set standards of performance and hold students accountable for the formulation of their own thinking about a case. Although intuitive learners do not harm clients, damage is done to students if they are not helped to think logically, to reflect, and to integrate theory with practice.

Experiential Learner

Behavioral characteristics. Experiential learners are sometimes described as "late bloomers" because they start slow and experience problems at the beginning of field placement. They seem unable to tap previously learned resources as easily as other types of learners do and may appear to operate in a vacuum. As a result, their tolerance for frustration is low and their self-confidence weak, especially in young, beginning students who experience additional problems with regard to achieving independence and who lack related work experience or have limited life experiences. Unlike the intuitive learners who cling to old ways of doing things at the beginning of placement, experiential learners are frequently unable to use past life and work experiences, even when field instructors are active and supportive in their teaching approach. In a graduate program wherein students usually have two different field-placement experiences, experiential learners often regress at the beginning of the second field practicum and act as though they had learned little from their first field experience.

During the first days of orientation, these students are confused about basic instructions. The instructor may even question these students' ability to comprehend or wonder whether their intellectual endowment is adequate. They may even be immobilized during the early weeks of field placement. In effect, these students are saying, "I must do before I understand." As their anxieties increase, they become self-focused, which in turn produces mixed results. On the one hand, these students attempt to rationalize their lack of progress or lack of response from clients; on the other hand, they begin early on to deal with self-awareness.

Experiential learners are overly dependent and need approval and recognition. They feel an urgency to obtain positive signs that they really can perform and place demands on the field instructor's time. Like intellectual learners, they look for a magical formula, although they are more attuned to feelings than are the intellectual learners and are more flexible in their response to structure. Their problems are similar to those of the intuitive learner with regard to conceptualization, but their problem-solving approach is far less creative than that of the intuitive learner. However, because they develop self-awareness early, these students recognize their need to overlearn. Experiential learners find it difficult to accept the fact that they are plodders and may not produce the same quantity of work as do many other students. Even after these students begin to work through some of their problems, they continue to demonstrate lack of originality in approach and planning and difficulty in conceptualizing.

Teaching approach. Field instructors should help experiential learners experience success early in the field-placement experience so that feelings of adequacy and safety are reinforced. Case selection, therefore, is extremely important. These learners, more than the other two types of learners, must be able to relate to the cases at the beginning of placement. Although they should not be assigned what is unrealistically referred to as a simple, uncomplicated first case (which so frequently occurs with beginning students), the hostile, aggressive client should be avoided until these students have sufficient theoretical knowledge and self-knowledge to evaluate the significance of the client's behavior. Repetitive experiences with similar types of clients will help these students evaluate and work through their reactions to new situations and ideas.

The relationship between the field instructor and experiential learner is critically important. Although the relationship between field instructor and student is an integral part of the helping process regardless of the student's learning style, this relationship is especially important for experiential learners because they integrate intellectual content slowly compared with the other types of learners. Probably the two most frustrating and difficult problem areas for field instructors with experiential learners are the development of techniques that will stimulate these students to use their abilities more creatively and to conceptualize. With regard to the former, the field instructor should help them think through various interventive goals and alternatives in a more expansive manner. Gradually, experiential learners will begin to tap previous experiences, plan more independently, and recognize the importance of using their experience and ability in a less rigid, stereotypical manner. Helping these students to conceptualize is a slow and tedious process that can best be accomplished by repetitive teaching in a nonthreatening manner. Improvements should be explicitly recognized. Unlike intellectual learners, whose performances are enhanced by increased time in the field, experiential learners benefit from an extended period of course content before entering the field.

Frequently, anxiety is equated with learning blocks or a lack of native intelligence in these learners. It is difficult to determine their capacity for stress prior to placement, although their anxiety reaction is easily identified. Identifying and defining this reaction helps them begin to overcome obvious blocks and to accelerate learning. Repetition of simple and basic instructions during orientation, accompanied with approval and support, is necessary. If problems persist, the field instructor should discuss the difficulties directly with the student and should explore with the student possible outcomes and solutions to facilitate more independent functioning. The field instructor must be alert to this type of student lest the student become quietly dependent and is sent into the professional world forever dependent upon supervision.

RELEVANCE FOR STUDENTS

Not only must field instructors identify students' patterns of learning, but students, too, must think about and examine the ways in which they learn. Social work education ranks self-awareness high on the list of educational priorities; understanding one's learning patterns is an important part of self-examination and self-discovery and helps develop self-awareness in the student. By so doing, students begin to connect how they learn with factors that contribute to or hinder achievement of their learning goals and ultimately their effectiveness with clients. Students must understand that some difficulties in learning are not unique to them as individuals and that these difficulties may be overcome. Also, they must learn to identify and appreciate their strengths.

Achieving Balance among Thinking, Feeling, and Doing

Educable students are aware that they must make changes in themselves. However, they may be frightened about what these changes involve and how to proceed. Describing the three general types of learners and the strengths and difficulties inherent in each helps students think about their own learning patterns. Universalization is a good technique to use with clients who are not ready to think about their own behavior; this approach is equally valuable with students.

All students must learn to balance thinking, feeling, and doing. Students usually lean toward one particular style. Students should become aware of the obstacles inherent in their particular learning style. Understanding the different learning approaches can help students become aware of the need to balance thinking, feeling, and doing and stimulate necessary changes. It can make learning more challenging and change less frightening.

SUMMARY

A review of learning patterns emphasizes the value of identifying and evaluating ways in which adults learn and can be an important aid to field instructors in assessing and utilizing the learning-pattern abilities of individual students. Analyzing learning patterns provides structure to teaching methods; field instructors are able to reinforce strengths and anticipate and deal with the obstacles students encounter. Learning becomes a more conscious process if instructors know how the students learn, what needs to be changed, and how change can be promoted through the learning/teaching relationship. Moreover, this teaching approach stimulates field instructors to be more consciously aware that (1) all students do not, cannot, and should not be expected to learn in the same way, (2) learning occurs in many different ways, (3) students may learn in a way different from that of the field instructor, and (4) the field instructor's social work knowledge, skill, and practice experience are necessary but not sufficient. In other words, field instructors must become educators in the full sense of the word.

Students find value in thinking about and examining their own patterns of learning. It increases their self-awareness, makes learning more challenging, and helps students achieve balance among thinking, feeling, and doing.

REFERENCES

1. Sidney Berengarten, "Identifying Learning Patterns of Individual Students: An Exploratory Study," *Social Service Review* 31 (December 1957): 407–17.

2. Neilson F. Smith, "Practitioners' Orientations to Knowledge and Conceptual Learning from Practice: Part I," *Social Casework* 47 (October 1966): 507–14; and "Part II," *Social Casework* 47 (November 1966): 590–96.

3. Pauline H. Hammond, "Patterns of Learning in Fieldwork," National Institute for Social Work Training, London, England, *Case Conference* 13 (July 1966): 83–88.

4. Catherine Peck Papell, "A Study of Styles of Learning for Direct Social Work Practice" (Ph.D. diss., Yeshiva University, New York, June 1978).

5. Gerald M. Gross, "Instructional Design: Bridge to Competence," *Journal of Education for Social Work* 17 (Fall 1981): 66–74; and David E. Hunt, *Matching Models in Education: The Coordination of Teaching Methods with Student Characteristics*, Monograph Series No. 10 (Ontario, Canada: Institute for Studies in Education, 1971).

6. Charlotte Towle, *The Learner in Education for the Professions* (Chicago: the University of Chicago Press, 1954), p. 396.

7

STUDENT VIEWS OF THE FIELD INSTRUCTOR

"What you are speaks so loud I can't hear what you say" may very well be said by students to faculty unless the person of the teacher is inspired by the spirit he is seeking to fan to flame in his students.

— *Ruth E. Smalley*

The relationship between the field instructor and student is probably the most important learning component in social work education. This close working relationship is not experienced in any other aspect of social work education. Clarification of respective roles, however, does not happen automatically and requires more than an intellectual discussion of the responsibilities of each. The relationship process takes time and, as with all productive relationships, investment on the part of each individual. Field instructors must attempt to individualize the learner, which includes understanding how students learn and how learning can be maximized for a particular student. Students, on the other hand, seek role models. They are not sure what to expect from a close supervisory relationship and may be afraid that their chosen career will be in jeopardy if the field instructor learns their true lack of knowledge and skills. In the student–field instructor relationship, many behaviors are similar to those that occur in any planned change process, that is, an ambivalence to change on the part of the student, a need to identify areas that require change, and a need to willingly commit to change. The field instructor begins at the student's current level of experience and ability, identifies and capitalizes on the student's strengths, instills trust, and provides the support and direction necessary for the student to make necessary changes.

REALISTIC AND UNREALISTIC VIEWS

In any relationship between two people, one looks for certain qualities in the other. Patients who require medical attention search for qualities in the physician that instill trust and hope. They want someone who is self-confident, knowledgeable, and can make decisions. Clients look for many of the same qualities in their social workers. Students, too, anticipate certain qualities in their field instructors that they believe will help them learn and develop their skills. These expectations, however, may not be altogether realistic, particularly in the beginning of the field-placement experience. Likewise, field instructors' attempts to meet these expectations may not be realistic.

Field instructors, particularly when they are new to the job, place considerable emphasis on being liked by their students and consequently often fail to confront their students' annoying behavior. In so doing, a field instructor's frustration and anger may be repressed to the point that when limits are finally established, they may be harshly enforced as if to undo the field instructor's leniency.[1] Thus a balance must be struck between what students want and what they need to become self-directed learners. It is not possible for field instructors to be liked at all times by all students, nor is it possible for field instructors to like their students at all times.

Students' resistance to changes in ways of thinking, feeling, and doing appear in various forms. Feelings may be projected on the field instructor or anger may be quite overt. At times the field instructor will appear to be unsupportive, difficult to please, unfeeling, or too busy to care. Because of the intensity of the students' placement experience, their relationship with the field instructors can be highly emotional. Field instructors may become a target for the students' feelings, admiration and respect, needs, and anger. Because field instructors invest in their own aspirations and wish to perform competently as teachers, they too are subject to questions and doubts.[2] Clearly, realistic and unrealistic expectations are involved in the student–field instructor relationship.

STUDENT VIEWS OF FIELD INSTRUCTORS

In a study of students' relationships with field instructors, students rated their field instructors in four areas of supervisory activity: emotional support, intellectual teaching, self-actualization, and power. Results indicated that the intensity of criticism of the field instructor was in part related to the phase of learning in which the student was involved; that is, students in their early years of training were more critical of their instructors than were students who had nearly completed their field training.[3] A study of 101 students revealed that first-year graduate students expressed significantly higher levels of criticism than did second-year students.[4] However, a follow-up on this study did not support the hypothesis that students' criticism of their field-instruction experience decreases with each level of learning. On the contrary, criticism by casework students increased with each phase of learning, and no clear-cut pattern emerged for group-work students.[5] This same follow-up study identified other factors that related to students' perceptions of field instruction, such as types of field instruction (individual or group), sex of the field instructor, grades, and so forth. Such studies are useful in providing direction for the improvement of field instruction in that they shift attention to the cognitive-structuring area in agency–school contacts by promoting faculty liaison–field instructor discussions, promote school-sponsored meetings for agency field instructors, encourage seminars on supervision, and point out the benefits of manuals and instructional materials provided by the schools. By knowing what material is being covered in the classroom, field instructors are able to adjust their level of expectation and exchange ideas and concerns with classroom faculty and other field instructors.

G. D. C. Woodcock studied the reaction of forty social workers to their first experience with field instruction.[6] Results indicated that field instructors were helped through their anxiety and what they viewed as a career crisis by good communication and continued guidance from the school and by the support and encouragement that they received from their agencies and administrators. Input from the educational institution helps stimulate field instructors to make necessary changes in their teaching methods, to become more clear about learners' needs, and to reinforce their commitment to the teaching–learning process.

Objectionable Behaviors in Field Instructors

Four supervisory behaviors that students consider objectionable were identified by Aaron Rosenblatt and John Mayer:[7]

1. *Not enough autonomy*: students felt supervision was constrictive.

2. *Amorphous supervision*: students felt supervision was too vague.

3. *Unsupported supervision*: students felt supervision did not allay anxieties or that it exacerbated fears and worries.

4. *Therapeutic supervision*: students felt supervisor looked for deficiencies in the student's personality. Students vehemently objected to "therapeutic supervision."

In contrast, Alfred Kadushin found that supervisees in social work practice were more willing to accept the therapeutic intrusions of the supervisor than were the supervisors to offer such help.[8] A possible reason for this is that practitioners have already achieved a measure of success in their chosen profession and do not have as much at stake as students do. Also, practitioners may be clearer about learning needs and may not feel threatened about "not knowing." Under such circumstances it is always easier for the supervisor to share feelings, reactions, and to look inward.

Helpful Qualities in Field Instructors

A group of undergraduate students were asked to identify qualities in field instructors that they believed helped them in the learning process. This question was included in students' overall evaluation of their field-practice experiences at the end of the second semester of the field-practice course. The results were tallied over a nine-year period.[9] Students consistently listed four qualities in field instructors that they found helpful: (1) knowledgeable about the profession, (2) supportive, (3) encouraging independence, and (4) available to students. The field instructor's confidence in the student's ability to achieve and his or her encouragement to develop one's own style were also rated high by students. These positive qualities correlate with the first three objectionable behaviors identified in the Rosenblatt and Mayer study: not enough autonomy, amorphous supervision, and unsupported supervision.

STUDENT VIEWS OF TEACHING METHODS THAT ENHANCE LEARNING

The same group of undergraduate students who identified field-instructor qualities were asked to indicate teaching methods that they felt could have enhanced their learning but were not available to them. The most consistent response in this area was a perceived need for more structure in the supervisory conference, especially during the first semester. Students stated that this structure would have helped them clarify roles and expectations. This response suggests that, despite the fact that expectations are clearly explained in the field-instruction manual and highlighted in a practice seminar, students need to negotiate these issues directly with field instructors and agencies. Six supervisory issues related to the actual teaching process should be shared early with students in order to bring structure to the negotiation: (1) the time and place of the supervisory conference, (2) the number and kinds of cases to be assigned, (3) information about agency policies and procedures, (4) content and process of the evaluation, (5) the nature of the supervisory process, and (6) the kinds of skills students will learn and their relevance to practice.[10] These negotiations incorporate both agency and school expectations and are made with the person(s) to whom students will be most responsible. In so doing, students are able to see that the agency and the school are working together.

Students in the nine-year study also indicated that more feedback from instructors about process recording would be helpful and that they expected a more critical analysis of their recordings. In a similar study, a group of supervisors and supervisees employed in social agencies were asked to select the satisfactions and dissatisfactions about which they felt most strongly.[11] Interestingly, one of the supervisees' dissatisfactions was that supervisors were not sufficiently or specifically critical of their work. The survey indicated that supervisees are anxious to do a better job and look to the supervisor for help in identifying the deficiencies of their work. Students are prepared for a critical analysis of their work; when this does not occur, they feel cheated.

During the nine-year period in which undergraduate students evaluated their field experiences, responses did not show students felt that the relationship had taken on therapeutic qualities,[12] which contrasts with Rosenblatt and Mayer's finding that graduate students objected to therapeutic supervision.[13] Most of the undergraduate students believed that they were free to express their feelings and concerns and that the field instructor encouraged openness. This discrepancy may relate to the fact that in graduate programs more emphasis is placed on the development of a relationship with clients and on the therapeutic implications for both client and student. Also, in the undergraduate study, this question was asked at the end of the field-practice course when at least some meaningful changes had occurred. In other words, in the undergraduate study, the struggle and hard work had paid off; thus negative feelings toward the field instructor generated along the way may have dissipated. Also, the students may have wanted and liked the therapeutic aspects of the student–field instructor relationship. Undergraduate students are open and eager to learn about themselves and may have less need to protect themselves than do many graduate students. However, it is not unusual for both undergraduate and graduate students to seek professional help as a result of the self-awareness gained through the field-practice experience; often they wish to share their feelings and reactions to this help.

STUDENT PERCEPTIONS OF THE IDEAL FIELD INSTRUCTOR

A two-year study of student perceptions of the ideal field instructor identified twenty-four characteristics.[14] Undergraduate, first-year graduate, and second-year graduate students were requested to rank these twenty-four characteristics in order of importance. Fifty-two undergraduate students who were currently enrolled in the second semester of a senior-level field-practice course participated in the study — a total of 85.2 percent of all undergraduate students in this course over the two-year period. The four most important characteristics of the ideal field instructor identified by the undergraduate students were (1) responsive to feelings and concerns of individual students, (2) supportive of students, (3) accessible and available for supervisory time with students, and (4) treats students fairly and objectively. The field instructor's ability to communicate theoretical and practice knowledge and to provide ongoing feedback on the student's performance were ranked fifth and sixth, respectively.

Low on the list of ideal characteristics were (21) focuses basically on professional rather than personal development of students, (22) sense of humor, seems to enjoy teaching, (23) allows experimentation with innovative techniques, and (24) participates in practice-related research. General satisfaction with field instruction was rated 5.3 on a 7.0 scale by undergraduate students.

The same undergraduate students who participated in the study by Stanley Piwowarski[15] also participated in the Urbanowski study of student evaluations of the field-practice experience.[16] In the Urbanowski survey, the four qualities of the field instructor that students identified as most helpful were among the top six ranked in the Piwowarski study. The lower rankings of the twenty-four characteristics concurs with the fact that these were seldom mentioned as helpful in the students' evaluations of their field instructors.

Although students did not emphasize the field instructor's sense of humor in the evaluation responses, they did mention it with some consistency. Thus, one might have expected "sense of humor" to rank higher than twenty-second on the list of ideal characteristics of field instructors. In addition, students were generally so positive about their field instructors in their evaluations that a higher rating than 5.3 might have been anticipated.

Value of Support

The need for support from the field instructor is clearly an important ingredient to learning in social work education. However, how and when to use support is contingent upon the skill of the field instructor. Tape recordings of student–field instructor communications in early conferences were studied by Judith Nelsen.[17] The tapes were examined in relation to the content of discussion, teaching/learning interactions, use of support by field instructors, and giving and requesting direction. In most tapes, support was used appropriately and most frequently in the first half hour of conferences. Following this period, students were freer to participate in conferences and to volunteer feelings. It was as if students felt free to express feelings after their anxieties about their performance with clients had been alleviated. It was noted that instructors offered higher overall levels of support to students who expressed more feelings. This support provided not only emotional reassurance, but also cognitive reinforcement for learning that helped students to consolidate understanding and move on.

Another interesting observation in this study of tape recordings was that students waited to hear what the field instructor would say and then requested further directions. The students questioned areas that were not covered by the field instructor or areas that were not clear from what the field instructor had said. This finding is important and possibly ties in with the finding that undergraduate students feel the need for more structure. Students invest a great deal in preparing for their conferences and want to use the allotted time to its fullest advantage. Their major preparation for conferences is the process recordings, and considerable time and effort go into these preparations, especially in the beginning of field practice. Thus it is natural that students would want to wait for feedback in the beginning of their conference that could provide a framework for the subsequent discussion. Field instructors who go off on tangents or expect students to begin their conferences with concerns and questions may find that students are more anxious and frustrated. On the other hand, students who are active at the outset of the initial conferences or who quickly ask questions and air concerns might be attempting to avoid focusing on the material prepared and may feel a need to control.

SUMMARY

Students expect certain qualities in their field instructors. Some of these expectations are realistic, whereas others are unrealistic.

All students look for qualities that are best suited to their own learning style. If these qualities are not available to them they may express anger, disappointment, and abandon the learning process. Field instructors also look for qualities in the learner that will blend with their teaching approach. Clarification of respective roles and compromises in expectations are frequently required.

Regardless of how teaching is approached, providing varying degrees of support throughout the learning experience is an important quality for a field instructor. In addition, the field instructor is viewed as a role model — someone who is knowledgeable about social work practice, willing to share this knowledge, and willing to permit students to observe him or her in action. Field instructors are expected to be open and honest and to provide positive feedback as well as constructive criticism. Availability of the field instructor is a quality that ranks high with undergraduate students, which appears to be directly related to the undergraduate student's need for extra support to make the required changes in thinking, feeling, and doing.

REFERENCES

1. Susan Matorin, "Dimensions of Student Supervision: A Point of View," *Social Casework* 60 (March 1979): 150–56.

2. Kloh-Ann Amacher, "Explorations into the Dynamics of Learning in Field Work," *Smith College Studies in Social Work* 46 (June 1976): 163–217.

3. Sheldon D. Rose, "Students View Their Supervision: A Scale Analysis," *Social Work* 10 (April 1965): 90–96.

4. Stanley Piwowarski, "Social Work Students: Phase of Learning and Intensity of Criticism of Field Instructors" (Social Work Department, Loyola University of Chicago, 1972); and Stanley Piwowarski, "Perceptions of an Ideal Field Instructor in Social Work" (Social Work Department, Loyola University of Chicago, 1979–81).

5. Sheldon D. Rose, Jane Lowenstein, and Phillip Fellin, "Measuring Student Perception of Field Instruction," in *Current Patterns in Field Instruction in Graduate Social Work Education*, ed. Betty Lacy Jones (New York: Council on Social Work Education, 1969), pp. 35–44.

6. G. D. C. Woodcock, "A Study of Beginning Supervision," *British Journal of Psychiatric Social Work* 9 (Autumn 1967): 66–74.

7. Aaron Rosenblatt and John E. Mayer, "Objectionable Supervisory Styles: Students' Views," *Social Work* 20 (May 1975): 184–89.

8. Alfred Kadushin, "Supervisor-Supervisee: A Survey," *Social Work* 19 (May 1974): 288–97.

9. Martha L. Urbanowski, "Summary of Student Evaluation of Field Practice Experience, 1976–1985" (Social Work Department, Loyola University of Chicago, 1976-1985).

10. Marion H. Wijnberg and Mary C. Schwartz, "Models of Student Supervision: The Apprentice, Growth, and Role Systems Models," *Journal of Education for Social Work* 13 (Fall 1977): 107–13.

11. Kadushin, "Supervisor-Supervisee."

12. Urbanowski, "Summary of Student Evaluation."

13. Rosenblatt and Mayer, "Objectionable Supervisory Styles."

14. Piwowarski, "Perceptions of an Ideal Field Instructor."

15. Ibid.

16. Urbanowski, "Summary of Student Evaluation."

17. Judith C. Nelsen, "Teaching Content of Early Fieldwork Conferences," *Social Casework* 55 (March 1974): 147–53.

8

VALUE OF FIELD-PRACTICE CRITERIA TO MEASURE PERFORMANCE

It is very important to recognize that progressive, cumulative, and definite stages and levels of learning have to be surmounted and specific knowledge and skills have to be mastered within set time periods.

— Max Siporin

Increased demand for accountability in the social work profession has raised questions regarding the need for a clear and explicit connection between the program's educational objectives and outcomes. Just as practitioners must be accountable for their performance with clients, schools must be able to demonstrate the readiness of their undergraduate-degree and graduate-degree students to perform competently in their profession. Developing ways and means to measure student performance not only demonstrates accountability, but fosters a high quality of professional practice in field settings.

Field-practice instructors in a social work program are in a strategic position to evaluate performance effectiveness. Student competence in working with people to enhance their functioning or to prevent crises is determined in field instruction. This task is difficult to accomplish without clearly stated criteria that identify and explicate practice behaviors to be achieved by all students upon completion of their practicum. These criteria reflect the social work program goals and objectives, the needs of community social service delivery systems and the Council on Social Work Education standards on accreditation. In addition, they are meaningful and useful to field instructors as a teaching tool and to students as goal-directed guidelines.

PURPOSE OF FIELD-PRACTICE CRITERIA

Field-practice criteria are necessary if one is to assess student performance in practice. More specifically, such criteria link the overall objectives of the social work program with specific knowledge, attitudes, and skills required for the various levels of professional practice. Criteria force schools to be clear about their goals, their relationship to social work education in general, and to the social services of the community. They are an important guide for students in assessing the progression of their learning and in achieving goals. Students can relate to the criteria and feel that the expectations are reasonable and achievable within a specific time span. Field instructors are guided by the criteria in teaching and assessing student performance in relation to expectations.

VALUE FOR STUDENTS

Many students enter the practice arena unprepared for a new and different approach to learning. Much is expected of them, and often they feel confused. Students want to look for guidelines, and they need to know what is expected of them. Field-practice criteria are valuable learning tools.

- They enable students to view the goals and objectives for the field-practice course as achievable over time, thus lessening anxiety and increasing motivation.
- They provide students with direction in the field-practice courses.
- They allow students to compare and evaluate their performance in relation to the criteria.
- They help students identify learning patterns easier and develop their own ways of meeting goals and objectives.
- They present an objective measure for determining a grade.
- They help students determine their readiness or suitability for social work practice.
- They help students clarify specific career goals.

VALUE FOR FIELD INSTRUCTORS

Social work schools no longer have the luxury of faculty field instructors; social agencies assume the responsibility for providing this important function. Although social agencies have many qualified social workers who are able to move into the teaching role, limitations exist. Often staff members are shifted within the sys-

tem, which results in changes in the field-instruction assignment. In addition, social agencies are experiencing financial cutbacks, which mean fewer social workers and increased work loads. Field instruction is time consuming, and the social workers who take on this responsibility often do so without being released from other assignments. Thus, if agencies are to assume this important role in the education of social workers, they need as much direction and support from the educational institution as possible. Field-practice criteria are a valuable source of support for all field instructors in that they facilitate the following:
- They enable field instructors to be more in tune with the objectives of the school's social work program and the behaviors that students are expected to achieve.
- They encourage field instructors to individualize learners.
- They guide and strengthen the teaching roles.
- They provide a base from which to formulate conclusions about the individual student's performance in specific areas and in various settings.
- They heighten objectivity in evaluating student performance and increase the degree of accuracy in assigning a grade to the overall performance.
- They promote a stronger link between social work education and agency practice.

CONTENT

The criteria should include content in the major areas of learning that describe expected performance for students at both undergraduate and graduate levels of learning. The major areas of learning include student functioning within the service-delivery system and various environmental systems, within the client system, as a learner, and as a member of the profession.[1] The following includes suggested content that may be translated into desired behavioral terms as required by individual programs and the student level of learning (See Chapters 9 and 10).

Functioning within the Service-Delivery System

Students should gain specific understanding of the structural and behavioral components of the community in which their field setting is located and of the ways in which these components influence their program and services. They must be able to interact with the various systems within the community in delivering direct services, be aware of the network of larger systems, and understand their effect on one another. Working relationships with community representatives should be established for the purpose of effecting social-system change, and a commitment to developing skill in evaluating issues and problems at the larger societal-systems level should be made. When it seems appropriate, students should be able and willing to assist in change or development in the delivery of service.

Functioning with the Client System

This content area should identify expected performance in relation to data collection and engagement of the client in the helping process; organization, synthesis, and analysis of data; structure and implementation of the intervention plan; and evaluation of intervention efforts.

Students must demonstrate their ability to explore factual information for accurate problem identification and to engage the client system in this process. They should identify client situations that are amenable to and profit from preventive intervention. Students should be able to perceive the social situation of their clients by identifying other individuals, groups, or larger systems involved in or affected by the problems; by increasing their awareness of the cultural, racial, religious, and gender factors relating to the problems and client system; and by broadening their understanding of the effect of community and social welfare systems on the problems. Students should be aware of the impact of their interactions with the client system and understand that the target of change may be a system other than the client.

Students must demonstrate ability to conceptualize and pull together facts in a clear and organized manner. They should be able to analyze the client-in-situation in relation to background information; effects of external elements in the problem situation; effects of cultural factors, racism, ageism, sexism, handicaps, and other biases on that situation; and the degree to which formal and informal societal resources have provided services to the client system. Students should develop skill in assessing the client system's ability to cope with stress produced by the problems and the defensive operations of the client system.

Students must be able to use an organized assessment to identify an intervention approach that will attain the stated goals and objectives. Students should help the client mobilize the resources of the client system in the process of achieving these objectives and involve other appropriate systems in the problem-solving process. They should be able to use these same principles of intervention in the area of prevention and be capable of offering appropriate support, reassurance, and feedback in providing for the needs of clients. Ability must be demonstrated in the use of interview or group-situation techniques to facilitate progress toward attainment of stated goals. Students should demonstrate their ability to deal with client termination, including the handling of their own response to separation.

Students must be able to evaluate the results of interventive efforts in relation to the client's capacity, their own roles in the helping process, agency services, and community resources. The process should be viewed as ongoing, and students must be flexible enough to reorder or change interventive approaches when it becomes necessary to do so.

Functioning as a Learner

This content includes the level of expectations for learning through the field instructor and pertinent others and the student's ability to assume responsibility for his or her own learning. Students should respond to and follow through on suggestions made by those in instructional and consultative positions. In this developmental process, students should demonstrate respect for the ideas and thinking of others and, in turn, share ideas and thinking with others in a constructive, helpful manner. Students should be able to transfer learning from one situation to another and to generalize learning so that it is transferable to other problem-solving endeavors. They should understand the value of recording for teaching and learning purposes. The recording should reflect the student's ability to use it as a tool to expand learning, develop skills, understand the client system, and conceptualize practice. Students should participate actively in the evaluation process by identifying patterns of learning, working on and through obstacles to learning, recognizing special skills, and focusing on areas that need to be developed.

Functioning as a Member of the Profession

Students should develop a clear understanding of and commitment to the goals, roles, functions, values, principles, and varied purposes of the social work profession. They should be able to use the values and basic principles of the profession as guides to behavior and realize the need for continued learning. Students should demonstrate their ability to evaluate their own roles with the client system and the effects of their feelings and attitudes on clients. They should be able to work with clients from a variety of backgrounds, cultures, handicaps, and so forth. They should be able to change their ways of thinking, feeling, and doing and work constructively with peers, clerical staff, social work staff, and individuals from other disciplines and professions.

SUMMARY

A set of practice criteria that identifies and describes the expected performance of students at the various levels of learning is an extremely valuable tool for determining the readiness of students to continue their social work education or establish their place in the professional practice world. Practice criteria allow all parties involved — student, field instructor, agency, school — to be clear about expectations, thus allowing energy to be invested in the attainment of the educational objectives.

Schools must be accountable for educating well-qualified practitioners and need guidelines for measuring the effectiveness of student performance. Agencies need to feel that they too have guidelines to which they can turn. To these ends, practice criteria provide a measure of direction, support, and security. The criteria can be an excellent teaching tool for field instructors by lifting their burden to develop a set of criteria that may only indirectly relate to the social work program's expectations and the individual student's learning needs. Field-practice criteria are especially valuable for students who need to be clear about goals and expectations. Students need a framework within which to operate, guidelines for using this framework, and a feeling of challenge and support as they move through the educational process. Field-practice criteria contribute positively to all of these goals.

REFERENCES

1. Margaret Dwyer and Martha Urbanowski, "Field Practice Criteria: A Valuable Teaching/Learning Tool in Undergraduate Social Work Education," *Journal of Education for Social Work* 17 (Winter 1981): 5–11.

9

SUGGESTED CRITERIA FOR UNDERGRADUATE FIELD-PRACTICE PERFORMANCE

There is a distinct need for clear specifications of anticipated practice outcomes for the preparation of all entry level professional social workers.

—Betty Baer and Ronald Federico

Identifying expected behaviors for students in field practice is important for all levels of social work education. It provides specific expectations for students' performance and a framework in which a plan can be established that will both improve the teaching of field instructors and achieve maximum student learning.

The following criteria cover two semesters of field practice for upper-division social work students. They expand on the areas of learning that were described in Chapter 8. Two important considerations should be kept in mind regarding this material: (1) These criteria cover learning experiences in a wide range of field settings; thus students' learning opportunities will vary. (2) Students have different backgrounds and life experiences and learn at different rates; consequently, unevenness in performance will be evident, particularly at the end of the first semester.

The second-semester criteria reflect progression of learning in all areas of the framework for generalist practice. It is expected that students will have more responsibility in the intervention with the client system; consequently, emphasis is on behaviors related to direct work with the client system during this semester. In addition, this section attempts to cover the client as individual, family, small group, organization, and community. Here again, students will not have identical opportunities with all client systems.

FIELD-PRACTICE CRITERIA FOR PERFORMANCE: FIRST SEMESTER

The following material describes the expected levels of performance to be achieved by the end of the first-semester field practicum. Areas of learning include the following:

1. *Functioning within the agency and community*: Structural components of the social agency system, operational procedures of the agency system, the community served by the agency, resource systems available to clients
2. *Work-load management*: Administration procedures, recording skills, organization skills
3. *Problem identification, assessment, and intervention*: Data collecting, assessing and planning for intervention, intervention with the client system, integration of theory
4. *Learning*: Responsibility for own learning, learning through process recordings, learning through field instruction
5. *Professional development*: Changes in ways of thinking, feeling, doing; management of feelings and attitudes; professional identification

Functioning within Agency and Community

Structural components of the social agency system. The student begins to understand the structural components of the agency as a whole, that is, the boundaries, linkages, hierarchy, and differentiation of tasks. At this stage of the learning process the student is able to do the following:

- Analyze and discuss agency structure from an intellectual approach and an external viewpoint, particularly if the student is attempting to understand a large bureaucratic system or has limited life and employment experiences
- Demonstrate detachment while attempting to find his or her niche within the structure and begin to apply the knowledge acquired in courses in social welfare policy and services
- Show interest in expanding knowledge, demonstrate curiosity about the operations within the structure, and feel comfortable asking questions

Operational procedures of the agency system. The student is able to demonstrate knowledge about the operation of the overall program within the setting. Although the operations may be vague and seem overwhelming, the student must be able to do the following:

- Identify and line up the actual and potential resources within the system that are available for various types of clients

- Relate to and be concerned about policies and procedures pertinent to the specific subunit within which he or she is involved
- Explain the basic policies and procedures to clients, community members, and representatives of other social agencies

The community served by the agency. The student struggles to relate the needs and demands of the community with what is available within the agency. The student is concerned about the at-risk population groups within the community and able to identify the service, resource, and allocation gaps within the geographic area and his or her own agency. The student begins to formulate conclusions based on relevant facts about the real and potential obstacles to groups who are discriminated against or disadvantaged.

The student is able to question appropriately the agency's involvement in changing or revising social policy as well as its attempts to keep current with community (local and broader) changes. The student demonstrates the following:

- Attempts to offer ideas and suggestions but may need help with an objective presentation
- Shows awareness of activities and programs in the community or agency that are concerned with decreasing discrimination and injustice
- May be actively involved with community groups working toward change

Resource systems available to clients. The student has demonstrated an eagerness to learn throughout the semester about resource systems available to clients:

- Has developed a good roster of social agency resources that would be helpful to clients
- Can discuss, with the field instructor, feelings of frustration or discouragement in dealing with problems encountered with the community resource systems

Work-Load Management

Administration procedures. The student understands the work performance expectations of the agency and is able to assume responsibility for following through on administrative procedures. Time sheets and statistical reports may create frustration, and the student may be critical about the time and energy invested in completing the necessary forms. In spite of this frustration, the student demonstrates the following:

- Accepts the need for such detail to facilitate the smooth operations of the program and completes such tasks with efficiency and accuracy

- Follows agency hours as a regular employee of the agency
- Understands the importance of the field instructor being informed of his or her whereabouts when not in the agency

Recording skills. The student's process recording has improved to the following point:
- Recordings are completed in a reasonable amount of time with a reasonable amount of effort.
- Recordings are turned in to the field instructor sufficiently in advance of the weekly conference to ensure study and evaluation by the field instructor.

The student is aware of the importance of prompt recording for agency purposes but still works on clear, concise written presentations while receiving direction, review, and feedback from the field instructor. The student demonstrates the following:
- Understands the necessity and value of recording for meeting the client's needs and for his or her own learning and professional development
- Drafts letters, memos, and reports in accordance with the regulations of the agency
- Rewrites letters, reports, and so forth less frequently

Organization skills. The student demonstrates organizational skills in the management of assignments:
- Shows good capacity to set priorities; initiates contacts within the agency on behalf of the clients; and follows through on suggestions, ideas, and information from these contacts
- Demonstrates ability to make community contacts related to the needs of the client and to follow through in meeting these needs

Problem Identification, Assessment, and Intervention

Data collection. The student has gained a theoretical understanding of the problem-solving process and begins to demonstrate the ability to apply this approach with clients. Although the student may lack consistent skill in this area, he or she shows good potential for continued development by demonstrating the following:
- Shows awareness of the importance of relevant information
- Begins to collect facts and to connect them with the problems and client situations that would be amenable to and profit from preventive intervention
- Shows awareness of the need to identify other systems involved in these with a fair amount of comfort
- Begins to see the relationship between the client and the problem situation (may tend to become fascinated with the intricacies and analysis of the problem *per se*)

Assessing and planning for intervention. The student begins to connect the presenting problems in the case situation with the underlying factors that are involved. Although the student overemphasizes the explicit or external factors, he or she, with some struggle, begins to organize the factual data and identify some of the underlying causes that created the current problem. More specifically, the student is able to do the following:
- Begin to identify some of the effects of societal attitudes toward differences in culture, race, life-styles, and the changing roles of women on the client system and the current problems
- Examine his or her attitudes, biases, and stereotypes
- Look for indications of how the client system has coped with the problem situation and initiate plans for intervention
- Assess the willingness of the client system to participate in the assessment process

Intervention with the client system. The student shows clear signs that he or she is able to use self appropriately in intervention with client systems by demonstrating the following:
- Capitalizes on development of observational skills and uses this skill effectively in client contacts
- Notes obvious discrepancies in self-report information such as physical appearances, behavior, and general interactions
- Listens to what the client brings to the interview, meeting, or encounter and is supportive in helping the client discuss the problem
- Functions within the organizational system adequately enough to help the clients know what is available to them

The student may be somewhat clumsy in explaining community resources to clients and in interpreting the client's special needs, problems, and situation to the appropriate resource system. He or she continues to be uncomfortable with the role clarification process, although it is becoming easier. If the client's need cannot be met within the agency or if supplemental help is needed, the student is able to perform the following:
- Seek out information regarding environmental resources
- Explore the complex systems within the environment (may be overwhelmed or confused by the operations of some)
- Help clients connect with resources that will help meet their needs

The student is also able to help clients feel comfortable discussing their problems by demonstrating the following:
- Conveys interest, concern, and capacity to identify with clients
- Shows willingness to learn about clients from different cultures, races, religions, or life-styles, despite discomfort in working with clients who are different from self

- Is aware of feelings and the role they play in working with clients
- Recognizes the need to be consciously aware of self in interactions with clients

Integration of theory. The student shows some indications that he or she is beginning to integrate theoretical content from classroom courses and readings:
- Realizes that theory can be applied but is unclear as to how to use it and may need considerable help in sifting out appropriate knowledge that applies to the clients and field setting
- Sees more meaning in the interrelatedness of systems to the client's behavior
- Is able to see the value of his or her theoretical orientation and principles in identifying potential problems but is not yet sure about their use in planning appropriate intervention

Learning

Responsibility for learning. Learning is a visible process for the student that is reflected in the following behaviors:
- Responds to new ideas and knowledge in a thoughtful, critical manner and attempts to incorporate this knowledge in work with clients
- Struggles to integrate theory from classroom courses and readings, although this effort may be superficially manifested
- Increasingly shares of ideas and appropriately questions the field instructor and appropriate others

Learning through process recordings. Process recording has proven helpful to the student's learning experience; it reflects the development of the following skills:
- More conscious awareness of self in contacts with clients
- Freedom to include own responses and feelings in the intervention process
- Begins to take responsibility for evaluation of his or her own strengths and for identifying areas that need to be developed
- Aware of protecting the confidentiality of clients

Learning through field instruction. The student has adjusted to field instruction as a method of learning/teaching:
- Roles are clearer although not entirely established.
- Student finds it easier to accept and use constructive criticism in the development of knowledge, skill, and self-awareness.
- Reinforcement and feedback from the field instructor are viewed as an essential part of the change process.
- Supervisory conferences are used productively; student follows through on ideas and suggestions resulting from conferences.

Professional Development

Changes in ways of thinking, feeling, doing. At this point it is extremely important for the student to demonstrate some capacity to change his or her ways of thinking, feeling, and doing. This frequently requires new approaches in "doing" as well as compromise. Although these changes may be difficult, the student shows evidence that these changes and adjustments can be made by demonstrating the following behaviors:
- Good relationships with peers and with professional and clerical staff
- Communication of needs and ideas to staff and working cooperatively with them for the good of the client.

Management of feelings and attitudes. The student begins to realize that his or her ideas and thinking are both valid and valued by demonstrating the following:
- Shows greater freedom in sharing ideas and becoming an active member of the professional team
- Begins to feel comfortable working with other professionals in the community (may tend to follow directions or agree because he or she feels unqualified to contribute to the plan)
- Discusses feelings with the field instructor and indicates willingness to risk with questions, ideas, and concerns as they relate to plans for the client

As the student continues to deal with the reality of the situation, he or she shows evidence of being in touch with feelings and attitudes regarding individual differences:
- Shows respect for clients as individuals
- Shows interest in learning about differences related to culture, race, gender, religion, and life-style
- Shows a desire to be more aware of own reactions and responses in dealing with clients in the helping process

Professional identification. The student becomes more realistic in terms of his or her concept of the professional person. Although the student shows a tendency to idealize the professional person, he or she needs direction and support in order to gain a clearer perspective of ethical practice considerations and the role of the professional social worker, including evaluation of both positive and negative performance.

The student demonstrates curiosity about professional associations and is interested in how they relate to the agency, client, and self. He or she may have joined a professional organization out of an awareness of shared professional commitments but is still not ready to participate in its professional activities.

FIELD-PRACTICE CRITERIA FOR PERFORMANCE: SECOND SEMESTER

The following material describes the expected level of performance to be achieved by the student by the end of the second-semester field practicum. Areas of learning include the following:
1. *Functioning within the agency*: Structure and function of agency, strengths and limitations of agency, work-load management, and relationship with colleagues
2. *Functioning within the community*
3. *Direct work with client system*: Problem identification; collection, organization, and analysis of data; selection and implementation of intervention plan; and evaluation of interventive efforts (feedback)
4. *Learning*: Learning through field instruction, field experiences, and professional and peer groups
5. *Professional development*: Commitment to professional values, continued awareness of societal problems

The behaviors described in the first-semester field practicum continue to develop and grow, resulting in better balance among thinking, feeling, and doing.

Functioning within the Agency
Structure and function of agency. The student begins to understand how the agency fits into the network of systems that are available to meet the needs of people. He or she better understands and appreciates the organizational dynamics within the agency and the factors involved in change processes. More specifically, the student demonstrates the following:
- Ability to see a relationship between the historical development of the agency and its current practices
- Comfort with the more commonly used policies and procedures and the ability to interpret them to client and community with unconstrained ease and conviction
- Ability to admit to the client that he or she does not know the answers to questions pertaining to policies and services as well as the ability to find the answers

Strengths and limitations of agency. The student is able to evaluate some of the strengths and limitations in the services provided by the agency and is generally constructive in his or her criticisms:
- Shows concern for the agency and a wish to contribute positively to its image and to enhance its effectiveness (at times may be unrealistic in expectations of the agency's meeting client needs)

- Integrates theoretical concepts dealing with social welfare policies and issues
- Develops an increasingly objective viewpoint and broadens his or her outlook on how a particular agency interrelates with other social agencies, community subsystems, and the profession

Work-load management. The student demonstrates an ability to manage his or her time by the following behaviors:
- Attendance and promptness in the office
- Makes and keeps appointments
- Plans for coverage when not in office
- Organizes assignments so that maximum services are provided for all clients
- Takes on a greater quantity of work and feels challenged by the increased complexity of the work load

Relationship with colleagues. The student's relationship with colleagues operates for the benefit of the client, and his or her relationship with the intervention system is open and honest:
- Shows a capacity to accept and use ideas and suggestions and can handle self in a constructive manner when disagreeing with directions or decisions
- Has a positive relationship with peers and is able to extend self, share ideas and thinking, and learn from others

Functioning within the Community

The student has expanded his or her knowledge of resources to meet the needs of people and realized that systems affect the lives of clients, as demonstrated by the following behaviors:
- Consistent in detecting obvious community problems and shows concern about them
- In some situations, establishes a working relationship with community representatives in efforts directed toward social-system change
- Recognizes the need to continue to develop skill in evaluating issues and problems at the larger societal-system level and has ideas about how and when to intervene at this level in the role of social worker or concerned citizen
- Works with the network of larger systems that impinge upon the lives of people — school, health, welfare, religious institutions, housing, or law enforcement — and more clearly understands how these interrelate to help or hinder growth
- Better understands the bureaucratic structure and function of these larger systems and demonstrates basic skill in utilizing their services for the benefit of clients

Direct Work with Client System
Problem identification.

1. *Exploration of factual information*: The student is aware that numerous factors influence the client/problem/situation and recognizes a need for help at this particular time. This awareness provides a measure of objectivity in determining the factors that are salient in the current client situation. The student is able to do the following:
- Take into account the physical and social conditions surrounding the situation and identify those involved in and affected by the conditions
- Specify potential members of the client system or those who will need to be brought into the problem-solving process

2. *Engaging the client in problem identification*: The student is sensitive to the emotional component inherent in any request for help and recognizes the importance of creating a climate that is conducive to exploring the client's request. The student:
- Identifies the seriousness or urgency of the situation fairly easily and acts on urgent problems without delay
- Recognizes the need to take into account the people who are viewing the social situation as problematic and clarifies how the client requesting the help perceives the problem
- Shows awareness that the problem issues related to the community and social welfare systems may have an influence on the client and the problem and that they also may be the target of change
- Actively helps the client identify the next step after the presenting problem has been clarified
- Involves the client in the decision to continue with the services of the agency or to use other environmental resource systems
- Clearly understands that this decision is based on the client's needs and wishes, the services available within the agency, and his or her ability to meet the client's needs

3. *Perception of human diversity*: The student considers the influence of culture, religion, handicap, sex, race, and life-style on the client's functioning and attitudes toward help. The values, attitudes, and behaviors of the larger societal systems related to minority and at-risk groups are contrasted with those of the clients. These factors are taken into consideration during the problem-identification process.

Collection, organization, and analysis of data.

1. *Development of data-collection techniques*: The student recognizes the importance of the scientific method of problem solv-

ing and has beginning skill in collecting facts about the client system; he or she is able to explore those areas that are relevant to the client situation. More specifically, the student demonstrates the following skills:

- Beginning skill in questioning the client in order to obtain appropriate information and in explaining the purpose of the interview and keeping it focused
- Observational skill to support and add to the knowledge about the client situation
- Conscious awareness of social interactions, physical appearances, and overt behaviors and ability to use these observations to objectively analyze the data
- Ability to seek out existing recorded material about the client system and synthesize it appropriately with factual data

2. *Organization of data*: The student is able to organize the facts in such a way as to facilitate evaluation and interpretation of their meaning. Reasonable inferences are made from the data; inferences are clearly distinguished from facts, as demonstrated by the following skills:

- Ability to perceive the connections among the client, problem, and the direction the worker takes in helping
- Awareness that multicausal factors influence the problem situation, ability to assess how the various systems involved affect one another, and ability to use this information both to understand the client and establish a plan for helping

3. *Analysis and assessment of data*: Student integrates and transfers theory from classroom courses and outside readings, although at times he or she may overinterpret the data or intellectualize without individualizing the client. The student is able to appreciate the dynamics involved in the client situation and begins to assess how the various elements are operating to maintain or promote the problematic situation. Specifically, the student demonstrates the following skills:

- Obtains appropriate background information about the client system and connects this with the current circumstances of the client
- Assesses those elements outside the client system that impinge upon or impose constraints on the situation: for example, societal responses to race, culture, gender, religion, and physical or mental states
- Recognizes and utilizes new support systems that become evident as the facts about the client and situation unfold
- Questions the degree to which formal and informal societal resources have provided or failed to provide services for the client

and analyzes those elements within the client system that are positively and negatively affecting functioning
- Draws from knowledge about the effects of stress on the system, whether this system be individual, family, or larger groups
- Assesses the client's personal capacities and coping abilities, strengths and weaknesses in the client's situation, and the requirements for improved functioning
- Recognizes some of the defensive maneuvers and mechanisms that are brought into play in dealing with stress and the effects they may have on the client's response to help

Selection and implementation of intervention plan.

1. *Use of assessment for establishing an intervention plan*: The student has developed beginning skill in articulating an intervention plan and can provide a logical rationale for the strategy. This strategy includes the following:
- A plan based on the data that have been collected and analyzed
- Goals correlated with the needs and capacities of the client system, services available within the agency, and the level of the student's capabilities
- Keeping the goals of the client paramount and examining them in relation to other systems involved in the change effort

2. *Approach to intervention*: The student is aware of the range of role relationships that are peculiar to the position of social worker. After the student and client have determined a suitable point of intervention, the student is able to use self in a variety of roles to facilitate change. These roles include acting as mediator, advocate, leader, agent of social change, broker, crisis intervener, and others as they are required to achieve intervention goals. In addition, the student is able to do the following:
- Establish and sustain the necessary work relationships required by the change process
- Recognize that in working with a variety of clients and other systems, the social worker assumes different role relationships
- Deal with the various influences, responses, and demands inherent in the diverse relationships

3. *Involving the client in problem solving and decision making*: The student is able to establish trust, begin at the point at which the client or other systems are experiencing the problem, negotiate differences, and communicate at the appropriate level.
- Helps the client become increasingly involved in the problem-solving and decision-making process, which requires continued clarification of the target system and the goals for change
- Further partializes the elements that require change and helps

the client system use the various resources and services that can be brought to bear on the target problems
- Uses advice giving, instruction, information giving, and other techniques as they relate to the established plan
- Appropriately supports the client system and offers reassurance and feedback as needed
- Accepts dependency and finds ways to help the client move toward independence
- Comfortably deals with expressed anger and hostility based on his or her increased understanding and appreciation of the meaning of such behaviors
- Challenges the client to action when appropriate

4. *Facilitating progress toward stated objectives*: The student understands the purpose in a given practice situation and prepares for each activity or interview as well as for the overall goals established with the client system. The student shows an ability to focus interviews, although this ability may not be consistently practiced. Specifically, the student is able to do the following:
- Respond quickly and easily to concrete and obvious psychological needs and provide for those needs through selective use of resources, adequate explanation of their use, and follow-up, when necessary, to assure that these needs have been met
- Anticipate the progression of content in working with a client and begin to plan for sequential groupings of meetings as opposed to focusing solely on single contacts
- Recapitulate with the client the progress made toward objectives and plan the next step for immediate and long-term actions

The student is able to question the client with greater sensitivity for the client's level of functioning and the objectives established to meet needs. Improved communication skills are reflected in the student's ability to do the following:
- Listen more effectively and include all members in the communication process
- Allow for the expression of feelings and control tendencies to rigidly follow a designated plan for helping
- Be aware of feelings involved in a given situation in relation to a particular subject matter and help the client modify these feelings when appropriate
- Begin to understand that feelings are related to values and past experiences and recognize that frequently the feelings and behavior exhibited by the client are a means of testing the worker's interest and willingness to help
- Risk, test intuitions, and assess results

Evaluation of interventive efforts. The student recognizes the need to evaluate the results of efforts to help and the importance of this for both the student's and client's learning. These skills are viewed as part of the scientific approach to problem solving and the need to be accountable for services offered to clients. The student and client evaluate the progress the client system has made toward the established goals and utilize this evaluation as a guide to continued intervention. More specifically, the student is able to:

- Actively engage the client in the evaluation process and identify achievements and goals that were not attained
- Analyze the gaps in agency policy in relation to the needs of clients and make appropriate recommendations regarding changes
- Honestly appraise own performance and recognize gaps in knowledge and skills that need to be expanded and developed
- Evaluate the community-resource systems, or lack thereof, in relation to the needs of clients and suggest possible solutions
- Show concern about social issues and social welfare policies that affect the lives of clients and demonstrate commitment to intervene to change or improve delivery of services

Learning

Learning through field instruction. The student recognizes the need to take responsibility for his or her learning by demonstrating the following behaviors:

- Submits recordings, summaries, and other written materials prior to conferences
- Prepares for instructional conferences by formulating questions and concerns
- Views written and oral skills as equally important, although one might be used more frequently
- Shows willingness to listen to, respond to, and follow through on suggestions
- Risks self by not being afraid to make a mistake (still cautious at times)
- Uses self independently by taking more initiative in the decision-making and planning processes, although he or she recognizes limitations
- Approaches intervention critically and thinks in terms of what might have been done rather than defending what was done
- Independently seeks answers to own questions by reviewing content from classroom courses and outside readings and persistently works to transfer theory to practice

Learning through field experiences. The student appreciates the focus and emphasis on learning. Repetitive experiences have

helped the student make comparisons and integrate learning with various situations. Specifically, the student is able to:
- Differentiate and recognize that all situations that require change cannot be resolved the same way
- Derive satisfaction from some assignments and attempt to understand his or her lack of satisfaction with others
- Question the reason for little or no change in the helping process, thus clarifying his or her role in the process and strengthening understanding of the dynamics that are involved
- Feel less threatened by those clients who are not amenable to help and view involvement with these clients as a challenge

1. *Development of recording skills*: The student uses recording as a tool to expand learning, develop skills, and understand clients. Recordings are organized, more selective, and completed with less effort. Although the student may still find recording a tedious and time-consuming task and summaries difficult to write, he or she is able to appreciate their learning value. This appreciation is reflected in the following behaviors:
- Reveals interaction with clients, feelings, and ideas in writing
- Integrates theory in recordings
- Pulls facts together and assesses the factual material in order to understand direction and goals in the problem-solving process
- Conceptualizes and shows potential for continued development of this skill

2. *Evaluation of learning*: The student begins to analyze the ways in which he or she learns and is aware of and able to talk about his or her more obvious problems that impede learning.
- Expresses desire to work problems through and efforts to do so are evident, although they may not be fully successful
- Recognizes the importance of changing ways of thinking, feeling, and doing, although he or she may still be fearful of these changes
- Views learning as an ongoing process and is aware of the need to be open to self-evaluation and the constructive criticism of others

Learning through professional and peer groups. The student's involvement in group learning is indicated by participation in group meetings, including general staff meetings, team meetings, and contacts with others in the unit.
- Usually prepares for the discussion, is willing to take responsibility for presenting material or ideas, and is constructive in responses
- Open to learning from other members of the team and other professionals and peers

- Incorporates some of the thinking and ideas that are presented and applies them to client situations

Professional Development

Evaluation of self. The student has developed awareness of feelings toward the client and recognizes how these feelings affect his or her ability to help. This awareness is especially evident in working with clients from different backgrounds, races, cultures, religions, and life-styles. The student is particularly aware of his or her tendency to overidentify and attempts to modify this. In general, the student demonstrates the following behaviors:
- More consciously aware of self when working with clients
- Recognizes the need for controlled emotional involvement and a more consistent attempt to avoid imposing own feelings, opinions, and values on others
- Clarifies career goals and realizes that the profession requires a commitment to ongoing learning in order to keep abreast of changes and directions within the profession.

Commitment to professional values. The student's values are in accord with those of the profession, and he or she is sensitive to the rights of clients.
- Shows willingness to take responsibility for own actions and does not become defensive when questioned about accountability
- Attuned to the principles of self-determination, confidentiality, and objectivity and feels strongly about the appropriateness of these principles as guides to his or her behavior

Continued awareness of societal problems. The student begins to use his or her knowledge base and experiences as well as professional literature and the mass media to become aware of social problems at the societal and community levels. The student is aware of the importance of professional organizations and is interested in exploring affiliations with such organizations.

SUMMARY

Based on the suggested criteria in field instruction at the undergraduate level, an evaluation instrument can be designed that uses a performance-rating scale, a narrative approach, or a combination of both (see Appendix D for example of evaluation instrument for second semester of undergraduate field instruction). An evaluation instrument that combines a performance-rating scale and narrative allows the field instructor to highlight a student's strengths and limitations and to identify goals for continued development.

10

SUGGESTED CRITERIA FOR GRADUATE FIELD-PRACTICE PERFORMANCE

> *The content of field instruction and the changes in student behavior that occur during the course are difficult to describe and assess, partly because of the problems of defining and observing the appropriate units of attention, and partly because of the difficulty of arriving at valid criteria for student achievement.*
>
> — Margaret S. Schubert

Graduate programs may organize their field practicum in different ways. They are influenced by their respective universities and social work communities and by the nature and objectives of their programs.[1] Consequently, criteria for performance in the field practicum vary in accordance with the educational thrust of the school, which makes it difficult to suggest universal criteria for the field component of graduate social work education. However, professional foundation content, defined as the knowledge, values, processes, and skills that have proven to be essential for the practice of social work, is common to all graduate schools of social work.[2] Advanced content builds on this foundation and relates to new knowledge and skills in the concentrations preferred by the school. Concentrations may be organized in various ways: fields of practice, population groups, problem areas, practice roles and interventive models, and advanced generalist practice.[3] Thus integration of professional-foundation content and specialized content must be demonstrated in the field-instruction courses.

Rosemary Reynolds described expected behaviors of the first-level student at the end of each quarter of the academic year.[4] She classified learning under the following categories: ability to form "meaningful" relationships with people, grasp of causative factors and ways of helping, self-awareness and self-discipline, and ability to fit into an agency setting and to think in terms of agency needs. Perhaps these categories are the base from which all other attempts have been made to identify learning expectations in the field-practice courses.

Annette Garrett discussed the problems and tasks involved in field training for caseworkers and established an early model for meaningful communication among schools, agencies, and students.[5] This model traced the process and sequence of field supervision through the fall, winter, and spring visits of the school liaison. She also demonstrated how students integrated learning in both class and field.

Margaret Schubert researched the field-work performance of first-year graduate students.[6] She attempted to establish performance standards for the field-practicum courses. Schubert later refined the scales developed through these studies and established criteria for assessing the graduate student's performance in the field practicum.[7] The University of Chicago School of Social Service Administration also developed standards for performance of the first- and second-year field-practicum courses.[8] The standards described in the University of Chicago and the Schubert publications are directed toward students preparing for casework practice. Both sets of standards have been used extensively and effectively within schools of social work.

Although much of the content from both sets of standards for the field practicum continues to be valuable, many changes have occurred in the professional community and in social work education. The Council on Social Work Education (CSWE) Commission on Accreditation established guidelines for professional-foundation content as well as for concentration areas and specializations in graduate education.[9] Currently, schools are more aware of the need for clear performance expectations in the field-practice component vis-à-vis educational expectations. Based on the educational objectives identified by the CSWE prior to 1984, Edith Schur and coworkers developed a specific set of field-education criteria for graduate social work.[10] They classified learning into five categories: setting, work management, practice, learning/supervision, and professional self. A sample portion of each section presented a progression of expectations over a four-semester period. These criteria reflect progress in identifying expectations for field-practice courses.

The following field-performance criteria are suggested for graduate students who are in direct practice with individuals, families, and small groups. The criteria stem from a common professional base but assume significant differences from criteria for undergraduate education in the levels at which content is taught and in the expected learning outcomes regarding conceptualization, integration, and performance. The levels that are described are in keeping with the tradition of two placements, usually in two practice settings — the first placement requiring 360 clock hours and the second requiring 540 clock hours. The goals of the first-level placement include integration of foundation content and build on this foundation through the application of knowledge, values, and skills with individuals, families, and small groups. The second-level placement emphasizes a higher level of abstraction in the application of foundation content that is enhanced by advanced concepts in work with individuals, families, and small groups.

FIELD-PRACTICE CRITERIA FOR PERFORMANCE: GRADUATE LEVELS

The following areas of learning are used to describe the expected levels of performance for graduate students:

1. *Functioning within the agency*: Structure and function of agency
2. *Functioning within the community*
3. *Direct work with the client system*: Problem identification; collection, organization, and assessment of data; selection and implementation of intervention plan (use of assessment for establishing an intervention plan, approach to intervention and involving the client, facilitating progress toward stated objectives, dealing with termination, evaluation of the interventive efforts)
4. *Learning through field instruction, field experiences, and professional and peer groups*
5. *Professional development*: evaluation of self, commitment to professional values

Functioning within the Agency

Structure and function of the agency. At the end of the first graduate field-instruction experience, the student should have a solid knowledge base of the structure and function of the agency. This knowledge base includes an understanding of the administrative hierarchy and the process of decision making at the local-agency level. The student is familiar with the history of the agency and understands its mission and goals. The student can make a connection between the agency goals, policies, and procedures and the services offered to clients. The student is able to explain services to clients and community members and implement these services in accordance with the needs of the clients. The student can organize his or her time and conferences with clients and can complete required statistical forms as well as other agency procedures that deal directly with client service. The student is aware of the inherent inequalities in social service delivery for special groups and recognizes when the rights of clients are violated. Action to resolve issues involving the rights of clients may not always be appropriate, but the client's welfare is the student's major consideration. The student is aware of both the strengths and limitations of the agency and criticism is goal directed. He or she is able to suggest ways to improve the services of the agency and does so cautiously and through the appropriate channels.

The student who completes the second level of field instruction assumes responsibility for continuous learning about the overall structure of the agency and for creatively using the resources within the setting. He or she has good basic knowledge about the operations of the larger and more complex social systems and knows how to use these systems for the welfare of clients. The student shows confidence in relating to colleagues in the agency. He or she can work reasonably well with a variety of different personalities and keeps clients' needs and professional values in the foreground. Although limitations within the agency may be identified, emphasis for the most part is on the strengths. Ways to contribute to changes in client services are explored and input is constructive and useful. The student is keenly aware when the rights of clients are violated and explores action to remedy such situations.

Functioning within the Community

Upon completion of the first level of field instruction, the student is cognizant of the cultural and racial diversity of the community and is reasonably comfortable in the community that is served by the agency. He or she is familiar with the major social service agencies in the area, has general knowledge about the operations of these systems, and can help link clients with services when appropriate. The student is aware that some client groups and their members are subject to social stress and are more at risk than others. He or she demonstrates concern about resources that are not available as well as the unmet needs of the community. The student expresses ideas about possible solutions to the dilemma but may not know how to follow through.

The second-level graduate student has a good understanding of bureaucratic structure and function of some of the larger, more frequently used service-delivery systems and is able to utilize their services for the benefit of the client. The student can work with the network of larger systems that impinge on the lives of clients and is able to act as advocate, linker, or consultant in relation to the needs of the client. In addition, the student constantly seeks to expand his or her own knowledge base. The student identifies the problems within the community and assesses the available resources to meet the needs of groups of clients. At times the student participates in actions to remedy these needs and in so doing examines the relationship among social, economic, and political conditions; social problems; and ameliorative effort.

Direct Work with Client System

Problem identification. At the completion of the first-level field instruction experience, the student is aware of the importance of different data for accurate identification of problems. He or she assumes responsibility for exploring the numerous elements that influence the client, situation, and environment, although the process may still be time consuming. The student is sensitive to the influence of handicaps, culture, sex, ethnicity, and race on the client system's functioning and attitudes toward help. The student is immediately responsive to clients' needs and is able to use appropriate techniques in establishing the beginning phase of the relationship, whether this be with an individual, family, or small group. The student is able to determine the extent of the needs and the direction of help, although he or she may experience problems helping clients who are nonvoluntary or who are not able to use traditional kinds of services. Nevertheless, the student demonstrates an intellectual grasp of the causative factors and an awareness of his or her own needs and expectations. Most students need to continue their emphasis in this area.

The second-level student is aware of the sources of data on the client system and impinging environmental systems and is able to collect this information within a reasonable amount of time, while focusing on clients' needs. The student uses self effectively in engaging clients in the process of identifying the problems or concerns and is not threatened or intimidated by client systems that are difficult to involve in this process. The student has a good grasp of the factors that may influence the client's behavioral responses, either positively or negatively. These factors include the effects of culture, religion, sex, ethnicity, race, and handicaps on the client system's functioning. The student is conscious of differences between his or her life-style and values and those of clients, of the stigmatizing attitudes within the larger social context, and of the ways in which these attitudes may affect the reciprocal roles in the helping process.

Collection, organization, and assessment of data. At the completion of the first level of field experience, the student recognizes the importance of a disciplined, organized approach to the helping process. He or she knows how to extract important factual content and organize it in such a way as to present a clear picture of the client system as it interacts with the environment. The student demonstrates organized thinking, and studies and assesses the reciprocal influence of the various systems on each other and the client system. The student recognizes the importance of connecting a knowledge base with the factual and observational content in order to make an accurate assessment. The student is able to assess the client/situation/environment in relation to the precipitating, causal, and underlying factors *vis-à-vis* the presenting problem. The student is aware of feelings that may be generated by issues of race, culture, religion, sex, and handicap. Current interrelationships and past experiences are viewed appropriately in relation to the present situation, needs of the client system, and intervention plan. The student demonstrates his or her beginning skill in assessment both orally and in written form. He or she still struggles to assimilate all the pieces into a clear, conceptualized assessment statement. The knowledge exists, but the student needs to practice and concentrate his or her effort before a more polished version is achieved.

The second-level graduate student functions consistent with the accomplishments described above. In addition, the second-level student has integrated the data collection, organization, and assessment processes into the helping approach and actively seeks knowledge for action, testing, evaluating, coordinating, and replanning. The student is able to collect, organize, and assess data quickly and accurately as well as confidently determine the goals and lengths of the intervention process. The student recognizes that development of skill is an ongoing process and is mindful of the adjustments that he or she may need to make in thinking and doing.

Selection and implementation of intervention plan.

1. *Use of assessment for establishing an intervention plan*: At the completion of the first level of field instruction, the student recognizes the interrelatedness of the intervention plan and the assessment and understands how to formulate this plan. The student can state goals that have been agreed upon between the student and client system and understands that these goals are based on client needs. In addition, he or she is able to determine the schema

for achieving these goals. The student continues to struggle with conceptualizing this content, but the steps of this process are clear to the student and are recognized by him or her as being more than an academic exercise.

The second-level student is not only clear about the steps in this process but is able to integrate these steps in his or her overall approach. The student can formulate appropriate goals, establish mutuality with the client system about these goals, and maintain a good sense of direction as to the ways and means to achieve the goals. Generally, the student is able to establish the intervention plan with consistency and ease.

2. *Approach to intervention and involving the client*: At the completion of the first level of field instruction, the student is able to determine a suitable point of intervention based on the goals and schema that have been identified. The student is aware of the various systems that influence the life of the client and the different role relationships that may be required with these systems. The student deals appropriately with the various influences, responses, and demands inherent in these diverse relationships. He or she is mindful of the similarities and differences in the phases of the relationship with client systems of various sizes. Although there are gaps and inconsistencies in the differential use of self, progress is evident. The student is aware of and can establish sufficient trust to involve the client in decision-making activities, begins where the client currently is, negotiates differences, and communicates appropriately. Although the student understands the similarities and differences in various models of intervention, he or she may continue to struggle with the differential use of self in the application of these interventive approaches.

The second-level student identifies and intervenes in the various systems impinging on the life of the client. He or she can use self differentially and appropriately with these various systems. The student is consistent in determining a suitable point of intervention and can direct the clients toward the established goals. The student is consciously aware of the meaning of the kinds of behaviors related to involving the client in the beginning phase of the relationship and the feelings these may engender in the worker. He or she helps clients work through their ambivalent feelings toward being helped and encourages them to take risks in the change process. Trust in the relationship is established through a conscious use of self and the use of appropriate interventive techniques. The student is consistent in selecting the appropriate intervention models in accordance with the problems, strengths, and needs of the client.

3. *Facilitating progress toward stated objectives*: The first-level student is able to handle feelings and behaviors that arise as the client system progresses toward goals. Although he or she may show inconsistencies in identifying these feelings and frustration in dealing with behaviors, the student is cognizant of what is occurring and tries to respond appropriately. Concrete needs are handled with ease, and the student is aware of the feelings that surround these needs. The student has a good repertoire of techniques, which are used consciously and appropriately. The student is able to deal with the client system's feelings toward agency and worker and is generally able to help the client system express feelings. The student's responses, questioning, and use of direct influence are usually consistent, fitting, and timely. Although the dimension of the middle phase of the relationship, whether the relationship be with the individual, family, or small group, is understood from a theoretical perspective, it is not always operationalized. Generally, the student is able to stabilize the roles of all concerned, look for changes in other parts of the client system, and encourage the client to participate actively and responsibly. He or she better understands the influence of his or her feelings and attitudes on the client; generally, these feelings and attitudes do not interfere with the client system's progress. The student may not be consistent in dealing with issues related to handicap, race, religion, culture, ethnicity, or sex.

The second-level student is able to identify and deal with issues at a feeling level early in the relationship. He or she understands that multiple feelings accompany the various unmet needs and concerns expressed or implied by the client. The student recognizes that the client's feelings may be associated with a significant person or experience in the past and considers these factors, as well as reality factors, in his or her response to the client. The student has a sense of competence in the use of self even though he or she may occasionally feel overwhelmed by the multiple problems and the complexity of the client system. The student is aware of the beginning, middle, and ending phases of the relationship and is able to guide the client through these phases toward completion of the helping process. The student recognizes special issues that may arise with differences in culture, race, ethnicity, religion, sex, and handicap and can skillfully manage these issues. The student is able to examine his or her responses and behaviors and works toward making necessary changes in thinking, feeling, and doing.

4. *Dealing with termination*: At the completion of the first level of field instruction, the student understands the principles and pro-

cedures involved in the termination process. He or she is aware of the feelings and behaviors engendered in this process on the part of both client system and student. Even though feelings are anticipated by the student, dealing with termination may be confusing at this stage because of the actual feelings that arise. The student has a theoretical grasp of the importance of evaluation of clients' readiness for terminating vis-à-vis relationship stages and issues but may experience difficulty in sorting out and dealing with these issues. Reflective discussions may be necessary to ensure that the student completes the termination process or the transfer of the client to another worker or agency.

The second-level student understands the termination process and is able to use self effectively during this phase of the helping relationship. The student is more open about his or her feelings and is able to handle these feelings and respond appropriately to clients' feelings and behaviors. The student recognizes that the ending phase of the relationship is crucial to the outcome of the intervention and is able to complete the termination process or transfer to another worker or agency.

5. *Evaluation of interventive efforts*: At the completion of the first level of field instruction, the student is able to step back and examine the extent to which goals have or have not been achieved, although he or she may not see all aspects of the change and may have overly high expectations. The student evaluates his or her role and client efforts but may tend to focus on what has not been accomplished rather than on the positive effects of the interaction. He or she is able to relate the problem-solving process with the research-design and evaluation processes that help strengthen a disciplined scientific approach toward helping.

The second-level student is aware of the need to evaluate the progress of the client system periodically and to make necessary changes or adjustments in goals. He or she objectively evaluates his or her role and is able to build on strengths and make necessary adjustments in thinking, feeling, and doing. The research point of view becomes important in terms of knowledge building and in evaluating practice with questions such as How do I know? What is the evidence? What consequences do these contacts with clients have on the impinging systems? How is change facilitated at the level of the agency and in the larger community in order to benefit clients?

Learning

Learning through field instruction. At the completion of the first level of field instruction, the student takes responsibility for his or her learning. Written recordings, tapes, and other materials for conferences are submitted sufficiently in advance for the field instructor to review them for teaching/learning purposes. In addition, the student prepares for the conferences with questions and concerns. The results of the field-instruction conferences are used constructively and reflected in client contacts and functioning within the agency and community.

The second-level student demonstrates the behaviors described above, although some regression may be evident at the beginning of the second-level experience. There is depth to the conference discussions; the student is able to share ideas and concerns and is willing to risk being wrong or off track. Conferences with the field instructor are productive and used in a growth-producing manner.

Learning through field experiences. At the completion of the first level of field practice, the student is able to learn from a variety of experiences, including differential use of self with various client systems, application of appropriate learning from one client situation to another, and use of different kinds of recording experiences. Although the student may not consistently learn from all experiences, he or she is aware of the value of these available resources. Both positive and negative awareness of the ways in which learning occurs are understood by the student. He or she willingly deals with learning obstacles when they are encountered.

At the second level the student more clearly understands his or her own patterns of learning and is concerned about making the necessary changes in order to maximize learning. The student is able to work with various client systems and connect learning from earlier experiences. He or she uses all available resources to promote learning and independently seeks out information about these resources. Various types of recordings are used for learning purposes, and the student recognizes those that are most helpful to his or her learning needs. He or she is prepared to use recording in future employment.

Learning through professional and peer groups. At the completion of the first level of field instruction, the student contributes to group meetings, including meetings and consultations within the agency and the community, although he or she may be somewhat hesitant to participate actively. The student understands that learning occurs through these experiences and responds positively to the suggestions and ideas of peers. He or she may be cautious in challenging or questioning the ideas expressed by others.

The second-level student feels free to share ideas with others, challenge and question colleagues, and present a rationale for his or her thinking. He or she actively participates in group meetings, demonstrates confidence in his or her knowledge, and utilizes consultation for ongoing development.

Professional Development

Evaluation of self. At the completion of the first level of field experience, the student is aware of the effects of his or her feelings, attitudes, values, and life-style on the client system, although he or she may not always be conscious of feelings, attitudes, and reactions during client contacts. The student is concerned about this lack and wants to develop self-awareness in greater depth. The student openly examines his or her feelings and their effects on client systems. He or she is able to control feelings when dealing with other systems and keeps the welfare of the client in mind. The student is able to evaluate his or her responses to colleagues and the professional community and to make necessary changes in approach.

At the second level the student is more consciously aware of the effects of his or her feelings on the client systems. He or she actively appraises self and usually determines areas that require change. The student is equally aware of the effects of his or her feelings on colleagues and significant others who are involved in the helping process and demonstrates an ability to control feelings and focus on the client's welfare.

Commitment to professional values. At the end of the first field-instruction course, the student is aware and accepts the values of the profession as defined in the National Association of Social Workers' Code of Ethics[11] and understands the importance of integrating these values in every phase of the helping process. Clarity about his or her own value system increases, and the student finds these values compatible with those of the profession. The student's behavior with client, agency, colleagues, and community is professional, which includes respecting the rights of all those involved in the helping process. The student takes responsibility for his or her actions and for the most part is not defensive when questioned about performance or professional behavior. The student is interested in the various professional organizations, although he or she may not be actively involved. The student is more aware of social issues that involve the profession as a whole, including relationship between the profession and social welfare.

The second-level student's performance is consistent with that described above. Professional values and ethics are well ingrained and reflected in the student's behavior and attitudes toward clients, agency, colleagues, and community, and commitment to upholding these values is demonstrated. The student is aware of the need for consistent renewal of the meaning of values and their application to ongoing practice. He or she is committed to promoting the goals of the profession, is concerned about the role of professional organizations, and is interested in making a contribution through these and other political, legislative, and community sources. The student is not only aware of social issues involving the profession as a whole, but is prepared to work on the resolution of ethical dilemmas within the profession and to work toward the promotion of social justice in the broader community. He or she understands the value of using the best knowledge available so that growth will continue. The student understands the connection between research in the development of practice theory and the contribution of social workers to practice theory and institutional change.

SUMMARY

Although criteria for performance in field practicum for graduate students vary, professional foundation content, defined as the knowledge, values, processes, and skills that have proven essential for social work practice, is common among all graduate schools. Whereas the goals of first-level graduate placement include integration of foundation content, second-level placement emphasizes a higher level of abstraction in the application of foundation content.

REFERENCES

1. Council on Social Work Education, *Curriculum Policy for the Master's Degree and Baccalaureate Degree Program in Social Work Education* (New York: Council on Social Work Education, 1984), Appendix 1, p. 8.

2. Council on Social Work Education, Commission on Accreditation, *Handbook of Accreditation Standards and Procedures* (New York: Council on Social Work Education, 1984), Section 7, p. 6.

3. *Handbook of Accreditation Standards*, Appendix I, p. 9.

4. Rosemary Reynolds, *Evaluating the Field Work of Students* (New York: Family Service Association of America, 1946).

5. Annette Garrett, "Learning Through Supervision," *Smith College Studies in Social Work* 24 (February 1954): 1–109.

6. Margaret S. Schubert, "Field Work Performance: Achievement Levels of First-Year Students in Selected Aspects of Casework Service," *The Social Service Review* 32 (June 1958): 120–37; and Margaret S. Schubert, "Field Work Performance: Repetition of a Study of First-Year Casework Performance," *The Social Service Review* 34 (September 1960): 286–93.

7. Margaret S. Schubert, *Assessment of Social Work Student Performance in Field Work* (Minneapolis: University of Minnesota, School of Social Work, 1966).

8. Aleanor Merrifield, Jan Linfield, Edythe Jastram, eds., *A Standard for Measuring the Minimum Acceptable Level of Performance in First-Year Field Work in Social Casework* (Chicago: School of Social Service Administration, University of Chicago, 1964); and Aleanor Merrifield and Sylvia Astro, eds., *A Standard for Measuring the Minimum Acceptable Level of Performance in Second-Year Field Work in Social Work* (Chicago: School of Social Service Administration, University of Chicago, 1969).

9. Council on Social Work Education, *Handbook of Accreditation*.

10. Edith Schur, Joann Barndt, and Jan Baum, "A Criterial Structure for Graduate Field Education: A Model for Planning, Performance, and Evaluation," *Social Work Education Reporter* 31 (May 1983): 6–10.

11. "Code of Ethics of the National Association of Social Workers" (New York: National Association of Social Workers, 1980).

11

THE ROLE AND USE OF THE FACULTY LIAISON

As the most continuous link between school and field, the faculty field liaison carries the major responsibility for making any field situation "work" once it has been determined that it satisfactorily meets the criteria for a suitable field site for students.

—Margaret Schutz Gordon

The faculty field liaison acts as the representative of the school who coordinates and consults with the agency administrator, field instructor, and student in regard to the needs and expectations of all parties involved in the education of the student in the field-instruction courses. The faculty liaison plays many key roles within this educational unit. He or she collaborates and negotiates with the agency administrator, instructs and confers with the field instructor, advises and advocates for the student, and serves as the link with the school field-planning team. The field-liaison function, however, is often neglected, overlooked, or may exist *pro forma*. The responsibilities of the field liaison may not be explicated clearly or become visible until a crisis, usually related to the student's performance, occurs.

NEED FOR AN ACTIVE LIAISON

During recent years, the need for finding an active, invested liaison has increased. In the past faculty-based field instructors were equally identified with the schools and their field-practice settings and were knowledgeable about their students' overall academic performance. Currently, however, this does not necessarily occur. The increase in the number of undergraduate and graduate students in social work education in the past ten years and the demise of faculty field units have resulted in a greater demand for agency placements with agency-based field instructors. Agency-based field instructors no longer feel that they can take more than two students because of the demands of their own client–agency assignments. For many field instructors, the pressures of their job permit only one student per agency field instructor. Schools respect and reluctantly accept this situation, even though it may mean negotiating with several field instructors in one agency. The responsibility lies with the school to bring the agency and school together in the teaching partnership and in demonstrating commitment to the students that their practice experience will meet their educational needs and stimulate them to achieve their potential.

Many schools are concerned about the function of the liaison role in the educational process because of the challenges involved and demands of time on faculty who assume this role. Some schools have hired faculty whose major responsibility is the liaison role. This has advantages and disadvantages. Although a full-time liaison is able to concentrate his or her efforts on the liaison function and does not become bogged down by classroom teaching demands and the broad concerns of the university, the liaison role becomes too specialized. The classroom faculty, however, may drift away from this important function, thus losing their identification with the practice world in which students are involved. Some schools have elected to assign most, if not all, faculty to the liaison role, which permits faculty members to be connected with at least some aspect of the field-practice component and to be in touch with the realities of the students' practice experiences. All faculty need to keep abreast of what is occurring in practice and to adjust their course content in relation to what is happening in the field. In addition, the liaison role helps faculty understand the demands of students' practice experiences and develop expertise in helping students achieve their overall goals.

REVIEW OF THE LITERATURE

Lydia Rapoport and Jona Rosenfeld focused on the liaison's role as advisor to student by identifying five specific purposes that relate to this role: (1) helping students acquire knowledge, (2) enlarging self-awareness, (3) integrating personal and professional values, (4) internalizing professional norms and controls, and (5) solving predicaments.[1] They suggest a framework for the advising process. More recently, articles have discussed the role and function of the faculty liaison to field-practice settings and beyond that of the advisor to students. Margaret Schutz Gordon discusses the role and activities of the field liaison. Emphasis is mainly directed to the liaison's relationship with field instructors and suggested ways to help field instructors develop their teaching skills.[2]

Amy Rosenblum and Frances Raphael examined the purposes and functions of the liaison. Their discussion focuses on the functions of the liaison as they relate to the agency and to issues dealing with school–agency relations, field instruction, and the students.[3] They present their thinking from the viewpoint of a full-time faculty field liaison.

Suanna Wilson lists seven specific role responsibilities of the faculty liaison.[4] Missing from her list, however, is the faculty liaison's role with the administrator of the field-practice setting. She identifies typical problems that arise in the relationship between field instructor and school and presents questions designed to stimulate discussions at field-instructor meetings. One problem that bears repeating is the infrequency of faculty liaisons' visits because of their numerous academic assignments.[5] Other professions such as nursing, medicine, and education maintain similar connections with the practice world in the education of their students. Both nursing and medical schools have well-staffed faculty who are directly connected with students during their clinical experiences — not dissimilar from the faculty-based field units in social work practice settings and the school–agency–community learning centers established by some schools of social work. In the field of education, practice teaching for students is somewhat similar in that the "cooperating teacher" is not a member of the full-time university faculty. A faculty supervisor is assigned from the university; he or she schedules a time to observe the student teacher in action. Ordinarily, the basic purpose of the supervisor's visit is to monitor and assess the progress of the student teacher's performance, identify specific areas of difficulty, offer assistance, and keep in touch with cooperating teachers and principals.[6] In other words, the primary responsibility of the university supervisor (liaison) lies with the student teacher. Lowell Horton and Karen Harvey suggest that a shift in emphasis from supervision of student teachers to the preparation of the cooperating teachers to assume more of the supervision and to become fully functioning members of the educational team would be beneficial. This shift includes spending more time in consultation with teachers as well as arranging for workshops and a course on the supervision of student teachers. Horton and Harvey feel that cooperating teachers should spend time on campus and be aware of the vital role they play.[7]

Although social work education has dealt successfully with some of these concerns, a need continues to exist for standardizing and refining the role of the faculty liaison. A recent survey of master's degree students examined factors associated with student satisfaction with field learning. Complaints about the liaison made up the largest category of negative factors in the experience.[8]

COORDINATING THE AGENCY–SCHOOL PARTNERSHIP

Since the dream of reinstating faculty-based field instructors appears to be in the far distant future, if it occurs at all, social work education must concentrate on coordinating the agency–school partnership and using currently available resources. Social agencies are rich in knowledge and skill; schools must tap and develop these resources so that everyone involved may benefit equally in the educational endeavor. One approach to this end is effective use of the faculty liaison. The liaison has a role with the agency administrator, field instructor, student, and director of the field-instruction program within the school.

Role with the Agency Administrator

Although faculty liaisons are not as actively involved with administrators of agencies as they are with field instructors and students, it is, nevertheless, crucial that their roles be clearly understood by the administrator. If a crisis or problem arises with a particular student, the administrator will likely become involved. If he or she is unclear about the responsibilities of the various parties, the outcome may be delayed or negatively affected. When field placements are new to the school, the liaison should involve administrators in the initial discussions so that mutual expectations can be shared and resources within the setting can be explored. In addition, administrators should be apprised of any major changes in the curriculum or administration of the school. Administrators must feel that they are a part of the educational team and should have the opportunity to express ideas and concerns about the specific field-instruction program and broader educational practice issues. The liaison should be responsible for sharing major educational issues that are raised by agency administrators with the school so that they may be further explored and discussed at school/agency administrator meetings. In other words, administrators have much to contribute and should be heard. They need to know something about the students who are placed in their setting. At the time of the placement, information should be shared about the student's background, including employment history, education, and potential as viewed by the school. The rationale for the placement selection should be stated either orally or in writing. Administrators should be apprised of students' progress as well as the performance of their field instructor(s). A written contract between the agency and the school may be part of the negotiations with administrators to clearly establish respective roles and expectations.

Role with the Field Instructor

The faculty liaison plays an important role with field instructors. The liaison–field instructor relationship is basic to helping field instructors develop teaching skills and become an actively involved member of the educational team. Contacts with a field instructor vary according to the teaching experience of the instructor and the needs of the students. However, all field instructors should know that the liaison is always available and have at least one consultation visit after each academic semester or quarter has commenced. Gordon points out the need for the liaison to monitor field teaching sufficiently enough to ensure that the school's requirements are met and to be able to offer help skillfully. The field liaison must continually remain current with the situation by offering help without hovering or pushing too hard and by doing far more than merely saying, "Call me if you need me."[9]

Field instructors who are new to their teaching role require more frequent contacts. Marion Bogo suggested that new field instructors meet in small groups with faculty on a bimonthly basis.[10] The faculty member who serves as group leader also functions as liaison for the instructors in the group and with their students. The small group meetings enhance the competence of field instructors and the quality of field education provided for students. In addition, this mechanism achieves greater uniformity in the interpretation of expectations of field instructors, students, and schools.

Contact with field instructors at the beginning of the field-instruction experience should provide field instructors with some information about students. The information shared should be similar to the materials shared with administrators but with greater focus on the anticipated learning needs of the students *vis-à-vis* backgrounds and experiences. Field instructors, both new and experienced, should be informed about the classroom content that is being taught. This information might range from discussion of the materials obtained at orientation meetings for new field instructors to an update of course syllabi for the experienced instructors. The liaison is responsible for keeping field instructors informed of any subsequent curriculum or administrative changes within the school.

Scheduled consultation visits should have structure so that time is effectively used. The following guidelines list the responsibilities of the liaison:

1. The faculty liaison initiates contact with the agency. However, the field instructor and administrator or both are expected to contact the liaison to discuss issues or concerns related to student learning, especially when difficulties are perceived.

2. The faculty liaison's visit to the agency should be arranged sufficiently in advance of the end of the semester to review, with the field instructor, the areas of learning that will be discussed with the student at the time of evaluation.

3. The faculty liaison reviews a selection of the students' recordings: process recording, case summaries, recordings for agency purposes, and other available teaching/learning materials. Strengths and obstacles to learning are discussed with the field instructor. Goals that enhance learning are identified. Plans to help the student deal with learning difficulties are formulated.

4. The faculty liaison meets with a new field instructor at the agency at approximately the midsemester point to discuss learning/teaching progress and concerns. A second consultation visit toward the end of the semester is encouraged; this visit is determined on an individual-need basis.

5. The faculty liaison meets with the student at the field placement or soon after the agency visit in order to share reactions and discuss the student's overall progress in learning. The liaison may have his or her own style of meeting with the student: for example, in a group with or without the field instructor or individually at the field-placement or school office.

The field instructor is responsible for the following:

1. The field instructor notifies the student of the liaison's visit. The field instructor discusses, with the student, the purpose of the visit and the general areas that will be covered. The student may be asked to participate at some point in the visit.

2. The field instructor makes the student's recording or other teaching materials available to the liaison. The recordings and other materials are up-to-date and include process and summary recordings, recordings for agency purposes, tapes, and so forth.

3. The field instructor prepares for the liaison's visit by reviewing the field-practice criteria in the manual and his or her progress notes on the student's learning.

4. The field instructor identifies the student's learning gains and the difficulties the student has experienced during the semester. The field instructor shares these with the liaison and is prepared to discuss ways in which the student was helped to overcome difficulties and the results.

5. The field instructor has formulated a plan to meet the ongoing learning needs of the student and the kinds and number of learning experiences that the field instructor will make available in order to achieve these goals. This plan should be shared and discussed with the faculty liaison.

6. The field instuctor arranges for the administrator or program director to be available to meet with the liaison if educational or agency concerns and questions arise or if educational developments or changes must be noted.

7. In the event that learning problems on the part of the student are indicated, the field instructor contacts the liaison immediately and arranges for a visit. The student is made aware of the concern and is available to participate in the discussion and educational planning.

Awareness of these assorted responsibilities takes the mystery out of the meeting, and energies may be directed toward developing the skills of both instructors and students. In addition, these guidelines provide a framework for the academic-term evaluation of the student.

The student's grade at the end of each academic term is jointly determined by the field instructor and liaison. Every effort should be made to come to an agreement on the grade; however, ultimate responsibility should rest with the faculty liaison. If the faculty liaison–field instructor relationship is based on openness and directed toward learning, discrepancy in determining students' grades seldom occurs.

Role with the Student

The faculty liaison is responsible for specific field settings. The liaison ordinarily advises, consults with, and acts as advocate in all academic matters for students in these field settings. Rapoport and Rosenfeld suggest that the role is determined by the student's educational needs, which are present in either manifest or latent form.[11] Students usually play a more active role in regard to their field placement and experiences. The liaison is usually the first person with whom students, particularly undergraduate and first-level graduate students, learn about, question, and react to their placement in terms of expectation, types of clients served, the community in which the setting is located, and the field instructor. Students relate to the enthusiasm and interest of the liaison in the description and should feel free to express their reactions to the agency, neighborhood, and so forth. It is not unusual for students to react with caution to inner-city placements and to state their fears about going into a particular community. If students have not been involved directly in the selection of their placements, they may have a negative reaction to or feel angry about some aspect of the choice. Feelings, concerns, and questions should be carefully handled and emphasis should be on the learning experiences and field instruction available. The liaison should prepare students for their interview and first contact with the field-placement agency. The agency administrator or field instructor should be involved in the discussion as to a particular student's readiness for the placement.

The role of the liaison should be clarified with students at the beginning of the academic year, even though this is done at orientation meetings and outlined in the field-instruction manual and even if the student has had prior experience with a faculty liaison. Once again, emphasis should be on the student's education and learning needs. The liaison–student relationship should be sufficiently comfortable for the student to be able to share impressions on the strengths and weaknesses of the agency, clients, and field instruction. If this dialogue is established early, communication breakdowns may be overcome if they should arise during the academic year.

Faculty liaisons should be available to students in planning for their second-level field-instruction courses or in discussing issues about employment and career planning. Some students may want to discuss their fears and anxieties about leaving the security of the academic environment and meeting the challenges of the professional world. A summation of their learning, with focus on strengths and areas for continued work, is helpful, even though such discussion is a part of their evaluations in the field-instruction courses.

Role with the Director of Field Instruction

The faculty liaison is responsible to the director of field instruction in matters relating to the field-instruction courses. The director, in turn, is usually responsible to a committee on field instruction and ultimately to the dean or chairperson of the department. The director is available for consultation on issues that may arise with students, field instructors, and agencies that cannot be resolved. If the issue threatens the continuation of a student in the placement role, the liaison should take the necessary steps in accordance with the policy established by the school. This action may begin as a consultative matter; if learning goals are not achieved, a decision-making body should be available to determine the individual student's future in social work education. It is unwise for the liaison to make a major decision without using all available resources in consultation with the agency and school.

The faculty liaison should apprise the director of field instruction in writing of the strengths and weaknesses of the field placements at the end of each academic year. The committee that plans for students' placements should know the kinds of learners who are most successful in a setting or with an individual field instructor. This consideration may avoid pitfalls in learning and teaching and helps keep strengths in the foreground.

If issues regarding field-placement settings or quality of field instruction occur, the director of field instruction and possibly the committee on field instruction should be advised and consulted about continuation of either. The liaison is responsible for identifying any concerns with administrators and field instructors and for clearly indicating steps that need to be taken to rectify the situation and the reason for withdrawal from the program if such action is warranted.

DEALING WITH PROBLEMS

Student problems should be identified early in the field-instruction courses. If students and field instructors are sufficiently comfortable to discuss issues with their liaison, major problems may be avoided. The only way the liaison can remain on top of the situation is through contact with the student or field instructor, preferably both. This contact need not be time consuming or a formal event. A telephone call to the field instructor after an appropriate interval or a casual encounter with the student may provide sufficient clues to warrant closer monitoring.

Rosenblum and Raphael have made important comments on the student–field instructor–liaison triad.[12] They refer to the pivotal position held by the liaison — the person who carries the authority of the university. In the event of problems, the position holds considerable power and attempts may be made to manipulate the respective relationships. The liaison must be able to maintain a neutral position and be as objective as possible if an educationally sound solution is to be achieved. Given the sensitivity of the liaison's position within the triad, it is essential that the liaison's movements be purposeful and based on clear, educational assessment to avoid iatrogenic consequences.

Procedure

The liaison must be supportive to both student and field instructor. Initially, the liaison should encourage the student and field instructor to share concerns with each other and understand the expectations of the other party. Frequently, students feel that they cannot share their concerns with the field instructor. If their concerns are appropriate, students must be aware of the procedure for dealing with problems. This procedure should allow for the following steps:

1. Student and field instructor share concerns with those directly involved.
2. If a solution cannot be reached, the liaison becomes involved.
3. After all facts are gathered, a three-way discussion is recommended so that all parties can hear one another and agree to the recommendations or plan.
4. In serious problem situations, these recommendations or plans may need to be distributed in written form to all parties involved.
5. If continuation of the student in the field placement is in question, the liaison is responsible for communicating the situation to the director of field instruction and for seeking consultation with other resources established by the school.
6. The determination for continuing the student in the field placement is made jointly by agency adminstration and the school. The final decision on educational matters is made by the school.

All parties are better able to deal with problems if they are identified and solutions are attempted prior to the final evaluation. In the event of disagreement during the evaluation, the field instructor should include a statement of the discrepancies or the student may choose to include an addendum to the evaluation. The liaison should be apprised of the disagreement and determine the seriousness of the issues. The steps listed above may be necessary.

Student Advising

Shankar Yelaja identified and discussed two major goals in student advising: professional education goals and personal development of the student.[13] It is not unusual for a wide range of personal issues to arise during the educational process. These issues can vary from financial needs to relationship issues that are stimulated by the content of the class and field-instruction courses. More often than not, these problems affect learning in the field-instruction courses. The liaison may need to act as an advocate for the student, as a link to resources, or as the presenter of facts to a faculty committee dealing with academic problems. Personal problems that interfere with learning in the field-practice course are usually identified through the field instructor–student relationship. These problems should be referred to the liaison as quickly as possible, lest the field instructor fall into the role of therapist. The liaison must clearly understand that his or her role does not include that of therapist and may need to make a referral for ongoing professional help for the student.

SUMMARY

The role and responsibilities of the faculty liaison should be explicated clearly. This faculty function is not effective unless it is valued by school administrators and viewed by faculty as being as important as other teaching assignments. Even though the faculty-liaison role is a vital component of the field-instruction courses, it is often neglected. It can be a time-consuming assignment, particularly if serious problems develop within the practice setting. On the other hand, the consequences are serious when these problems are not resolved adequately or, even worse, bypassed.

Faculty liaisons play an active role with field instructors and students. Although their role with agency administrators may not be as active, it is no less important. The faculty liaison is a vital link between the practice setting and school. Throughout the twentieth century, schools and agencies have discussed the need for a mutually beneficial partnership; thus far neither party has been completely satisfied with the arrangement. A satisfactory relationship cannot occur without both parties being well informed about the standards, operations, and needs of the other. A skilled, interested, and committed faculty liaison is informed about academic matters and course content; knowledgeable about the realities of agency practice; and able to work creatively, smoothly, and objectively with all parties involved.

REFERENCES

1. Lydia Rapoport and Jona M. Rosenfeld, "The Nature of Student Advising in Social Work Education," *Applied Social Studies* 1 (1969): 113–24.

2. Margaret Schutz Gordon, "Responsibilities of the School: Maintenance of the Field Program," in *Quality Field Instruction in Social Work*, ed. Bradford W. Sheafor and Lowell E. Jenkins (New York: Longman, 1982), pp. 118–22.

3. Amy Frank Rosenblum and Frances B. Raphael, "The Role and Function of the Faculty Field Liaison," *Journal of Social Work Education* 19 (Winter 1983): 67–73.

4. Suanna Wilson, *Field Instruction: Techniques for Supervision* (New York: Free Press, 1981), pp. 12–15.

5. Wilson, *Field Instruction*, pp. 266–68.

6. Marilyn Cohn, "A New Supervision Model for Linking Theory to Practice," *Journal of Teacher Education* 32 (May–June 1981): 26–30.

7. Lowell Horton, and Karen Harvey, "Preparing Cooperating Teachers: The Role of the University Supervisor," *Peabody Journal of Education* 57 (October 1979): 56–60.

8. Ann E. Fortune et al., "Student Satisfaction with Field Placement," *Journal of Education for Social Work* 21 (Fall 1985): 92–104.

9. Gordon, "Responsibilities of the School," p. 119.

10. Marion Bogo, "An Educationally Focused Faculty/Field Liaison Program for First-time Field Instructors," *Journal of Education for Social Work* 17 (Fall 1981): 59–65.

11. Rapoport and Rosenfeld, "The Nature of Student Advising," p. 119.

12. Rosenblum and Raphael, "The Role and Function of the Faculty Field Liaison," pp. 70–71.

13. Shankar Yelaja, "Student Advising in Social Work Education," *Journal of Education for Social Work* 8 (Winter 1972): 64–70.

ANNOTATED BIBLIOGRAPHY

The selected bibliography represents a review of past and recent social work literature on field instruction and field learning. The majority of the materials were published within the past two decades. A few earlier publications are included because of their significant impact on field instruction. The following cover basic field-curriculum issues, the practice/education partnership, varying levels of student learning, development of field curricula, and research studies.

ARTICLES

Amacher, Kloh-Ann. "Explorations into the Dynamics of Learning in Field Work." *Smith College Studies in Social Work* 46 (June 1976): 163–217.
   This article reports the results of a study designed to assess the learning process of four first-year students in field practice and their supervisor. The results indicated that all four students learned in multidimensional ways. The author stresses that supervision would be advanced by achieving greater flexibility in style.

Bartlett, Harriet M. "Responsibilities of Social Work Practitioners and Educators toward Building a Strong Profession." *Social Service Review* 34 (December 1960): 379–91.
   Variations in the functions of professional service and the education of professional practitioners are criticized. The need for establishing joint responsibilities and working together for the good of the profession is highlighted.

Barnat, Michael R. "Student Reactions to the First Supervisory Year: Relationship and Resolutions." *Journal of Education for Social Work* 9 (Fall 1973): 3–8.
   The impact of the intensive supervised experience is discussed with focus on three relationship areas: therapist stereotype, supervisor, and client.

Behling, John, Caroletta Curtis, and Sara Ann Foster. "Impact of Sex-Role Combinations on Student Performance in Field Instruction." *Journal of Education for Social Work* 18 (Spring 1982): 93–97.

The authors discuss an empirical study designed to test the impact of sex-role combinations of students and field instructors on the evaluation of students' field-placement experiences. The research findings imply that same sex-role combinations generally have a more positive effect on student performance than do different sex-role combinations.

Berengarten, Sidney. "Identifying Learning Patterns of Individual Students: An Exploratory Study." *Social Service Review* 31 (December 1957): 407–17.

Individual learning patterns of students in field work are studied. Three patterns in normal learners emerge: the experiential–empathic, the doer, and the intellectual–empathic. Descriptive data about these patterns, the dynamics of the students learning, and teaching methods are presented.

―――――. "Educational Issues in Field Instruction in Social Work." *Social Service Review* 35 (September 1961): 246–57.

Berengarten examines the issues and problems confronting the field instructor, the training agency, and the graduate school. The amount of time and effort invested in the field course *vis-à-vis* the class curriculum is explored.

Berkun, Cleo S. "Women and the Field Experience: Toward a Model of Nonsexist Field-Based Learning Conditions." *Journal of Education for Social Work* 20 (Fall 1984): 5–12.

A project designed to develop a model for nonsexist field-based learning is presented. The analysis is based on a systems approach and the identified barriers to nonsexist field experiences. Suggested changes are discussed.

Bogo, Marion. "An Educationally Focused Faculty/Field Liaison Program for Full-Time Field Instructors." *Journal of Education for Social Work* 17 (Fall 1981): 59–65.

This article describes and analyzes a program designed to provide new field instructors with the opportunity to learn a conceptual framework for viewing education in the practicum and to assess their new assumptions, approaches, and behaviors in this new role. The use of regular small-group meetings between field instructors and faculty is viewed as an effective model for educational and agency linkage and support needs of beginning field instructors.

Bruck, Max. "The Relationships between Student Anxiety, Self-Awareness, and Self-Concept and Student Competence in Casework." *Social Casework* 44 (March 1963): 125–31.
The major emphasis of this study is on determining the relationship between certain personality components and student competence in field practice. The extent to which students who have limited self-awareness, excessive anxiety, or who are immature can still adequately utilize their educational experience is discussed.

Clemence, Esther H. "The Dynamic Use of Ego Psychology in Casework Education." *Smith College Studies in Social Work* 35 (June 1965): 157–72.
This article explores the ways in which the students' background, stages of development, defenses, and learning styles affect classroom and field-work learning. An example illustrates how the field instructor can assist the student in integrating personal experiences and field-work training to become a competent practitioner.

Cohen, Jerome. "Selected Constraints in the Relationship between Social Work Education and Practice." *Journal of Education for Social Work* 13 (Winter 1977): 3–7.
This article highlights issues of concern about gaps between social work education and practice as identified by both educators and practitioners.

Dana, Bess S., and Mildred Sikkema. "Field Instruction — Fact and Fantasy." *Education for Social Work, Proceedings: Twelfth Annual Program Meeting* (New York: Council on Social Work Education, 1964).
This article focuses on concerns about the application of a curriculum-building methodology to field practice; the development of field instructors as teachers; and the administrative aspects of field instruction.

Dea, Kay L. "The Collaborative Process in Undergraduate Field Instruction Programs." In *Undergraduate Field Instruction Programs: Current Issues and Predictions*, ed. Kristen Wenzel (New York: Council on Social Work Education, 1972), pp. 50–62.

The author reviews four traditional patterns of field instruction from an historical perspective. The author proposes a transactional model for field instruction that assures that programs will be responsive to the unique and changing configuration of political, economic, social, and cultural spheres in which agencies and universities operate.

Downing, Ruppert A. "Bridging the Gap between Education and Practice." *Social Casework* 55 (June 1974): 352–59.

Several important questions are raised regarding the relationship between schools and agencies in their joint effort to educate students for professional practice. Central to bridging the gap is the establishment of partnerships that provide for mutual service and educational input. A description of a training center project demonstrates ways in which the school–agency relationship can fulfill commitments to both service and education.

Duncan, Minna Green. "An Experiment in Applying New Methods in Field Work." *Social Casework* 44 (April 1963): 179–84.

The experiences of a field-work instructor in implementing an innovative plan with students are presented. Two teaching methods are discussed: direct observation of client/worker interviews and student group meetings.

Erlich, John L., and Jesse F. McClure. "The Grassroots Ivory Tower." *Social Work* 19 (November 1974): 653–55.

The schism between practice and schools of social work is explored. Available strategies to remedy this problem are suggested.

Foeckler, Merle M., and Gerald Boynton. "Creative Adult Learning-Teaching: Who's the Engineer of This Train?" *Journal of Education for Social Work* 12 (Fall 1976): 37–43.

The teaching/learning process is compared to the functioning of a railroad system that includes a variety of situations, roles, functions, processes, and interactions. In using this analogy, the authors suggest that the educational system should utilize innovative and creative teaching to meet the needs of the adult learner (the engineer).

Fortune, Anne E., Candace E. Feathers, Susan R. Rook, et al. "Student Satisfaction with Field Placement." *Journal of Social Work Education* 21 (Fall 1985): 92–104.

A survey of master's degree social work students examines factors associated with student satisfaction with field agency, field instructors, and field learning. Relevant learning experiences and supervision are considered the most important factors in a student's satisfaction with field work.

Frumkin, Michael L. "Social Work Education and the Professional Commitment Fallacy: A Practical Guide to Field–School Relations." *Journal of Education for Social Work* 16 (Spring 1980): 91–99.
The need to establish and maintain viable agency–school relationships is stressed. The article presents an overview of this relationship, including a review of the field-education literature. A framework for understanding and improving agency–school relations from a systems perspective is presented.

Garrett, Annette. "Learning Through Supervision." *Smith College Studies in Social Work* 24 (February 1954): 3–109.
Garrett's classic discusses the process and sequence involved in field practice and establishes an early model for communication among schools, agencies, and students.

Gitterman, Alex, and Naomi Pines Gitterman. "Social Work Student Evaluation: Format and Method." *Journal of Education for Social Work* 15 (Fall 1979): 103–108.
In this study, agency-based and faculty-based field instructors identified role strain that emerged from difficulty with defining evaluation criteria, analyzing student practice, writing the formal evaluation, and helping the student accept the evaluation. A model for the content and process of student evaluation is presented.

Gould, Robert Paul. "Students' Experience with the Termination Phase of Individual Treatment." *Smith College Studies in Social Work* 48 (June 1978): 235–69.
The author reviews the literature on the topic of termination and reports on a study designed to determine how students managed termination. Recommendations are to anticipate termination with clients at the beginning of treatment and to perceive termination more as a growth experience than as a trauma.

Hamilton, Gordon. "Self-Awareness in Professional Education." *Social Casework* 35 (November 1954): 371–86.

Hamilton discusses three levels of self-awareness that should emerge during field practice and demonstrates their use by both students and field instructors. The three levels of self-awareness are students' ability to see themselves in the role of worker, to recognize their own unresolved problems, and to understand how these problems affect their ability to help others.

Hammond, Pauline H. "Patterns of Learning in Fieldwork." *Case Conference*, National Institute for Social Work Training, London, England, 13 (July 1966): 83–88.
 The authors describe some of the patterns of learning that are universally manifested when individuals approach new knowledge and new experiences. The need for field instructors to understand their own approach as well as students' responses to learning is stressed.

Hawthorne, Lillian, and Dorothy Fleisher. "A New Look at Laboratory Training in First-Year Field Education." *Arete* 11 (Spring 1986): 44–53.
 The authors describe a sixteen-hour laboratory training program to assist first-year graduate students enter into the field-instruction courses. The program proved helpful in orienting students to the field experience, preparing them for an initial interview, and alleviating initial anxieties.

Kagle, Jill Doner. "Restoring the Clinical Record." *Social Work* 29 (January–February 1984): 46–50.
 This article suggests ways to improve the clinical record. The author recommends that both classroom teachers and field instructors should teach generic recording skills and supports the notion that field students should use the narrative summary style of recording, as well as audiotapes and videotapes, early in their practical training.

Kendall, Katherine A. "Selected Issues in Field Instruction in Education for Social Work." *Social Service Review* 33 (March 1959): 1–9.
 The issues, problems, and questions that are posed are reflections of the experience of the first Educational Secretary and later Executive Director of the Council on Social Work Education. The topic areas include the rationale for understanding patterns of field instruction; the purposes, goals, method, and content of field instruction; and issues of dual responsibility.

Kettner, Peter M. "A Conceptual Framework for Developing Learning Modules for Field Education." *Journal of Education for Social Work* 15 (Winter 1979): 51–58.

An alternative to structuring field learning in order to achieve greater precision in teaching and learning is explored. Problem and possibilities of this design are discussed. A comparative analysis of field instruction of thirty-five graduate schools of social work is included.

Kolevzon, Michael S. "Evaluating the Supervisory Relationship in Field Placements." *Social Work* 24 (May 1979): 241–44.

The intensity of the supervisory relationship is discussed in terms of accountability; role in the transmission, assimilation, and application of values, knowledge, and skills to professional practice.

Leader, Arthur L. "An Agency's View toward Education for Practice." *Journal of Education for Social Work* 7 (Fall 1971): 27–34.

An agency executive analyzes myths that have persisted about classroom teaching and field-instruction agencies and suggests ways to overcome differences.

Matorin, Susan. "Dimensions of Student Supervision: A Point of View." *Social Casework* 60 (March 1979): 150–56.

The shift that the social worker must make from practitioner to field instructor is examined. Various aspects of student supervision are discussed. Field instructors are encouraged to continue to develop practice skills.

Mayer, John E., and Aaron Rosenblatt. "Sources of Stress among Student Practitioners in Social Work: A Sociological View." *Journal of Education for Social Work* 10 (Fall 1974): 56–66.

An exploratory study based on students' autobiographical accounts of their sources of anxiety is examined. Findings indicate that students' stress is aggravated by the simultaneous impact of their unrealistically high standards and tendency to blame themselves when they fall short of their goals.

Meyer, Carol H. "Integrating Practice Demands in Social Work Education." *Social Casework* 49 (October 1968): 481–86.

The need to develop new ways to incorporate the demands of practice into the structure of professional social work education is discussed. Competencies that a group of students achieved through a particularly desirable field-instruction learning experience are described.

Nelsen, Judith C. "Teaching Content of Early Fieldwork Conferences." *Social Casework* 55 (March 1974): 147–53.
Tape recordings of conferences between field instructors and students held early in the placement of graduate social work students are studied and discussed by the author. Findings from this study suggest that supervisors' techniques, students' responses, and content of discussion are mutually related and that the field placement setting influences all three. The study further illustrates that field instructors give more support to students who express more feelings and give more directives to students who request direction.

_____. "Relationship Communication in Early Fieldwork Conferences." *Social Casework* 55 (April 1974): 237–43.
The author uses tape recordings of conferences between students and field instructors to define, analyze, and discuss the teaching/learning relationship between the field instructor and student. Findings suggest the importance of an active mutual communication process and that supervision, like other forms of direct practice, is a measurable process.

Price, Hazel G. "Achieving a Balance between Self-Directed and Required Learning." *Journal of Education for Social Work* 12 (Winter 1976): 105–12.
Adult learning concepts and principles and educational issues from the viewpoint of schools are selected and analyzed. The uniqueness of the adult learner and the various roles of the field instructor are discussed.

Raskin, Miriam. "A Delphi Study in Field Instruction: Identification of Issues and Research Priorities by Experts." *Arete* 8 (Fall 1983): 38–48.
This three-phase national study on field instruction uses the Delphi technique to identify the research needs or issues in field instruction. Top priorities for further research are identified as (1) testing for the attainment of special skills, (2) appropriate learning objectives for different levels of students, (3) attributes of effective professional and learning experiences, and (4) the place of planning for field instruction in the overall educational and curriculum planning process.

Rose, Sheldon D. "Students View Their Supervision: A Scale Analysis." *Social Work* 10 (April 1965): 90–96.

This study explores the characteristics of students' reactions to supervision and ascertains the meanings of these reaction. Results show that the intensity of students' criticism of the supervisor is in part a function of their phase of learning.

Rosenblatt, Aaron, and John E. Mayer. "Objectionable Supervisory Styles: Students' Views." *Social Work* 20 (May 1975): 184–89.

On the basis of biographical accounts collected from second-year graduate students, four kinds of supervisory behavior that students considered objectionable are identified: constrictive, amorphous, unsupportive, and therapeutic. Students tended to cope by spurious compliance, concealment, and manipulation. Constructive steps to improve the situation are noted.

Rosenblum, Amy Frank, and Frances B. Raphael. "The Role and Function of the Faculty Field Liaison." *Journal of Education for Social Work* 19 (Winter 1983): 67–73.

This article is written from the perspective of a faculty field liaison. It defines, describes, and distills the essential aspects of the liaison role and clarifies the requirements for effective practice.

Schmidt, Teresa M. "The Development of Self-Awareness in First-Year Social Work Students." *Smith College Studies in Social Work* 46 (June 1976): 218–35.

This article reviews a study of the learning process of first-year social work students. Special emphasis is given to the place of self-awareness in the learning process.

Schur, Edith, Joann Barndt, and Jan Baum. "A Criterial Structure for Graduate Field Education: A Model for Planning, Performance, and Evaluation." *Social Work Education Reporter* 5 (May 1985): 6–10.

A process to help field instructors and graduate students achieve the CSWE curriculum objectives as they relate to field education is suggested. The specific learning objectives are arranged in outline form and divided into a four-semester developmental progression. The significant benefits of the process to students, field instructors, and school personnel are reviewed.

Schutz, Margaret L., and William E. Gordon. "Reallocation of Educational Responsibility among Schools, Agencies, Students, and

NASW." *Journal of Education for Social Work* 13 (Spring 1977): 99–106.

The authors argue that the lines of accountability among schools, agencies, students, and professional organizations seem dysfunctional in that they do not strengthen the incentives necessary to improve practice. A proposed reallocation of responsibilities that would improve the functioning of all elements of the education–practice system is recommended.

Tropman, Elmer J. "Agency Constraints Affecting Links between Practice and Education." *Journal of Education for Social Work* 13 (Winter 1977): 8–14.

The author reviews some of the inherent constraints within agencies that complicate or interfere with the achievement of an ideal relationship between agency goals and educational objectives.

Urbanowski, Martha L. "Recording to Measure Effectiveness." *Social Casework* 55 (November 1974): 546–53.

This article examines the purposes and objectives of recording in both social work education and practice as well as ways that recording can be used as a constructive tool for the worker and the agency. Three stages of recording are considered for the learner: process, combining two or more interviews, and orientation for practice.

Wijnberg, Marion H., and Mary C. Schwartz. "Models of Student Supervision: The Apprentice, Growth, and Role Systems Models." *Journal of Education for Social Work* 13 (Fall 1977): 107–13.

Three models of student supervision — the apprentice, growth, and role systems models — are explored from an historical perspective. The structure and process of the role systems model are examined; the authors believe that this model exerts a critical influence on student learning.

BOOKS AND MONOGRAPHS

Astro, Sylvia. *Guide to the Content of Second-Year Field Teaching in Casework.* Chicago: The School of Social Service Administration, The University of Chicago, 1961.

The focus of this publication is on the generic content taught in second-year field-work teaching. Specific areas that are covered include study, diagnosis, planning, treatment and essential concomitants of casework. The appendix provides a brief statement on field teaching methods.

Baer, Betty L., and Ronald C. Federico. *Educating the Baccalaureate Social Worker: Report of the Undergraduate Social Work Curriculum Development Project.* Cambridge, Mass.: Ballinger Publishing Co., 1978.

This book addresses the range of minimal activities, the basic practice competencies essential for all graduating baccalaureate social workers, and curricula content areas essential to the achievement of practice competencies.

Baer, Betty L., and Ronald C. Federico, eds. *Educating the Baccalaureate Social Worker: A Curriculum Development Resource Guide,* vol. 2. Cambridge, Mass.: Ballinger Publishing Co., 1979.

The focus of this volume is on the development of baccalaureate programs. The major areas covered include the various systems involved, education for practice competence, and the development of curriculum content.

Briggs, Thomas L., Gerald M. Gross, and Marion Wijnberg. *Field Instruction: New Perspectives on a Partnership.* Syracuse, N.Y.: Monograph Series published by Syracuse University School of Social Work, 1977.

This monograph presents three major papers offered in a series of five seminars for new field instructors. The paper provide a perspective on planning for and implementing field-instruction programs.

Council on Social Work Education. *Field Instruction in Graduate Social Work Education: Old Problems and New Proposals.* New York: Council on Social Work Education, 1966.

The papers published in the the monograph reflect three different emphases in the 1960s to the problems and potentials of field instruction. The common theme of the papers stresses the need for the improvement of the quality of field instruction as a component of social work education.

_____. *The Dynamics of Field Instruction: Learning Through Doing.* New York: Council on Social Work Education, 1975.

This collection of eleven articles on graduate and undergraduate field instruction is written primarily by directors or coordinators of field-instruction programs. The volume is divided into five sections and covers practice and interdisciplinary seminars, a field-instruction model for social administration, a student-designed practicum, and the role strain on both agency- and school-based field instructors. Of special note is the presentation on the practice seminar in social work education.

_____. Commission on Accreditation. *Handbook of Accreditation Standards and Procedures*. New York: Council on Social Work Education, 1984.

This handbook contains standards and interpretive guidelines for baccalaureate and master's programs: the field practicum, selecting agencies for the practicum, selecting field instructors, and evaluating student learning in the practicum.

Family Service Association of America. *Trends in Field Work Instruction*. New York: Family Service Association of America, 1966.

This compilation of eleven articles reprinted from *Social Casework*, 1955–65, provides a state-of-the-art overview of the instruction during this period. Areas covered include the supervisor's educational diagnosis of the second-year student's individual needs and pattern of learning; the relationship between student anxiety, self-awareness, and self-concept and competence in fieldwork; teaching through conjoint interviewing of clients by the supervisor and student; and a structured guideline for student process recordings.

Granger, Jean M., and Signe Starnes. *Field Instruction Model for Baccalaureate Social Work*. Syracuse, N.Y.: Monograph Series published by Syracuse University School of Social Work, 1982.

This monograph defines a working model for the development and maintenance of field-instruction programs at the baccalaureate level. A theoretical base and practical guidelines describe the main elements involved in field instruction: the interrelationships among and between these elements, experiences students should have, educational objectives, and behavior that demonstrates undergraduate-level generic social work expertise.

Hamilton, Nina, and John F. Else. *Designing Field Education: Philosophy, Structure, and Process*. Springfield, Ill., Charles C Thomas, 1983.

The major portion of this book focuses on the learning contract. It provides the rationale for the use of the contract as well as how it can be used to facilitate communication in field learning.

Jones, Betty Lacy, ed. *Current Patterns in Field Instruction.* New York, Council on Social Work Education, 1969.
This compilation of articles selected from major papers presented at the CSWE Annual Program Meetings includes selections on teaching and learning in the field, the evaluation process, practice methods, and agency settings. An overview of field instruction and a discussion of the administration of field instruction are also provided.

Kagle, Jill Doner. *Social Work Records.* Homewood, Ill.: The Dorsey Press, 1984.
This book stresses the importance of record keeping in social work practice and suggests guidelines for selecting and organizing information for the case record. The chapters on content and structure are helpful for field instruction.

Kirlin, Betty A. *In Search of a Consistency Model for Evaluation of Student Performance in Graduate Education for the Social Professions.* Lexington, Ky.: University of Kentucky, College of Social Professions, Monograph No. 2., 1974.
This monograph discusses the evaluation process, both in its planning and implementation stages, based upon a theory of adult learning and the knowledge, values, and goals of social work education.

Manis, Francis. *Field Practice in Social Work Education: Perspectives from an International Base.* Fullerton, Calif.: Sultana Press, 1972.
An integrated approach to field teaching at the graduate and undergraduate levels in the United States and in a number of developing nations is presented. Emphasis is on cultural factors and their impact on social work practice. Suggestions for change, reference sources, and a wide range of examples are also presented.

_____. *Openness in Social Work Field Instruction: Stance and Form Guidelines.* Goleta, Calif.: Kimberly Press, 1979.
The author stresses that students are better able to think for themselves and contribute creatively to their own learning when they have a stake in their own development, have the benefit of specific guidelines, and experience an atmosphere of openness. A six-stage model includes arranging a contract; determining stu-

dent tasks; deciding on student recordings; analyzing the student's work; discussing the student's evaluation; and writing the student's evaluation. Guidelines for each stage are provided.

Merrifield, Aleanor, Jan Linfield, and Edythe Jastram, eds. *A Standard for Measuring the Minimum Acceptable Level of Performance in First-Year Field Work in Social Casework.* Chicago: The School of Social Sevice Administration, The University of Chicago, 1964.

A committee composed of faculty and agency personnel who participated in field instruction developed a schedule for performance to be used as an evaluation tool, a guide to teaching content, and in the orientation of new field instructors. The appendices include the schedule and instructions for its use.

Merrifield, Aleanor, and Sylvia Astro, eds. *A Standard for Measuring the Minimum Acceptable Level of Performance in Second-Year Field Work in Social Work.* Chicago: The School of Social Service Administration, The University of Chicago, 1969.

This monograph is a sequel to *A Standard for Measuring the Minimum Acceptable Level of Performance in First-Year Field Work in Social Casework.* Members of a committee representing various types of specialized settings and various methodologies of casework, group work, and community organization set minimum graduate standards for any student, regardless of methodology or mixture of methodologies. The schedule consists of sixty-eight items of performance that can be evaluated.

Rehr, Helen, and Phyllis Caroff, eds. *A New Model in Academic-Practice Partnership: Multi-Instructor and Institutional Collaboration in Social Work.* Lexington, Mass.: Ginn Press, 1986.

This compilation of papers covers a thirteen-year experiment in social work education. The project was designed for practitioners who planned to enter the health care field; however, the findings are applicable for the field in general.

Reynolds, Bertha C. *Learning and Teaching in the Practice of Social Work.* Silver Spring, Md.: NASW Classic Series Edition, 1985.

This classic in social work literature was first published in 1942. In addition to historical social work content, the book includes excellent material on learning and teaching in social work education. The chapters on the supervison of practice are particularly meaningful for field instructors and students in the practicum courses.

Rothman, Jack, and Wyatt C. Jones. *A New Look at Field Instruction.* New York: Association Press, 1971.
This book is the product of a three-year comprehensive study of the community organization curriculum in graduate social work education sponsored by CSWE. Several guiding principles and recommendations for implementing an integrated approach to field instruction are proposed.

Schubert, Margaret S. *Assessment of Social Work Student Performance in Field Work.* Minneapolis, Minn.: University of Minnesota School of Social Work, 1966.
This booklet presents an instrument designed to describe and rate students' levels of performance in field placements wherein casework with individuals and families is the primary method used.

Sheafor, Bradford W., and Lowell E. Jenkins, eds. *Quality Field Instruction in Social Work.* New York: Longman, 1982.
The authors and editors wrote chapters specifically for this publication that deal with important issues in and the multiple dimensions of field instruction. This comprehensive overview includes a history of field instruction; objectives; selection and development of learning tasks; evaluation of teaching and learning; and the rights and responsibilities of parties involved in field instruction. An annotated bibliography is included.

Shulman, Lawrence. *Teaching the Helping Skills: A Field Instructor's Guide.* Itasca, Ill.: F. E. Peacock, 1983.
This monograph is drawn directly from the author's 1982 text, *The Skills of Supervision and Staff Management.* The material focuses on teaching basic cummunication skills and provides a base for monitoring and evaluating the development of these skills for beginners in field practice.

Skolnik, Louise. *Final Report: Field Education Project.* Washington, D.C.: Council on Social Work Education, 1985.
The Council on Social Work Education initiated a special one-year Project on Field Instruction to explore issues and needs and to identify problem-solving mechanisms to support and enhance field instruction. The project's activities were guided by a Technical Assistance Group, comprised of bachelors of social work and masters of social work faculty and agency personnel. This monograph contains information from two surveys, provides a

current assessment of field education in social work, and suggests areas for further development.

Timms, Noel. *Recording in Social Work.* London and Boston: Routledge and Kegan Paul, 1972.
The first part of this book reviews the historical observations on the recording process. The second part deals with the major objectives of recording — namely service, teaching, and research. It also discusses practical problems and considers future directions. The appendix provides examples of recordings.

Wenzel, Kristen, ed. *Curriculum Guides for Undergraduate Field Instruction Programs and Undergraduate Field Instruction Programs: Current Issues and Predictions.* New York: Council on Social Work Education, 1972.
The Council on Social Work Education, in collaboration with the Veteran's Administration, sponsored a demonstration project that led to the publication of this two-volume set. Volume 1 addresses specific issues relative to the early development of undergraduate field instruction programs. Volume 2 presents curriculum guides from four field-instruction models that are helpful in developing an undergraduate program.

Wilson, Suanna J. *Recording: Guidelines for Social Workers.* New York: Free Press, 1980.
The author offers a practical guide that describes how to use records creatively in teaching, learning, and practice. The text discusses the purpose, mechanism, and the various methods of recording. A special section addresses computerized, problem-oriented, and statistical recording. Other features include special readings on confidentiality and privileged communication and a topical bibliography.

_____. *Field Instruction: Techniques for Supervisors.* New York: Free Press, 1981.
This book provides a basic review of field instruction at both the undergraduate and graduate levels of social work education. Attention is given to the techniques of recording, monitoring and evaluating students' performance, the relationship between agency and school, and the accreditation process. The author recommends the use of an educational contract as well as a school–agency contract. The book provides many case examples, teaching aids, and exercises as well as an extensive bibliography.

APPENDIX A
SAMPLE PROCESS RECORDING

Student: The student is a twenty-four-year-old woman. She has a bachelor's degree in sociology and two years of experience in the Peace Corps. The process recording reflects her first experience in a social service agency.

Setting: Family Outreach Center

Client: Mrs. G, age twenty-four years, mother of K, age three years, daughter

Mrs. G and her three-year-old child were deserted by her husband six months ago. She is unemployed and currently receives AFDC, which is her only means of support. Mrs. G is new to the city and is not aware of the available resources related to employment and child care. She expressed apprehension about leaving her child with a neighbor who has offered to care for the child while Mrs. G is at work.

Mrs. G's brother is temporarily living with Mrs. G and her daughter. Mrs. G is concerned because her brother is not employed due to a job-related injury and therefore is not contributing toward the rent. Mrs. G's brother has applied for unemployment benefits. Mrs. G feels isolated and fearful in the large city. She cannot manage expenses on her current income and requests help in finding other resources.

FIRST INTERVIEW, 10/25

Purpose
To meet Mrs. G, to elicit her feelings about the situation, to clarify whether Mr. D (brother) is still living with her and her daughter, to discover the extent of Mrs. G's financial problems, and to explore other needs.

Observation

I made an appointment for 1:00 P.M. but due to a mix-up went at 11:00 A.M. in hopes of rescheduling our appointment. The client's phone was disconnected. Mrs. G lives in an apartment complex in what appeared to be a largely black community. The apartment building was sturdy but dingy looking. Mrs. G answered the door in her nightgown, and I explained that I could not make the 1:00 P.M. appointment but wanted to reschedule it, if we could, for later that afternoon. Mrs. G invited me in, saying that "this time was as good as any."

The apartment was spacious, nicely furnished, and very neat and clean. The dining room had apparently been converted into a bedroom for K; the bed was made, and the house seemed to be in order. The furnishings were adequate — a couple of pictures on the walls, ashtrays on the coffee table, a very "homey" and comfortable atmosphere. Mrs. G had apparently just gotten out of bed, so naturally was not yet "put together." She is a very pretty black woman, with a warm and friendly smile. K was still asleep in the mother's bedroom.

Content

I began by introducing myself. I explained who I was and that I worked in a service unit at the Family Outreach Center. I explained that I could see her on a weekly basis if she so wished and that the purpose of our meetings would be to work on any difficulties that she was currently experiencing. She told me that her only current problem was lack of money. Her rent was recently increased, K needs winter clothes, and she just cannot meet expenses on her current income. She told me that she had spoken to a Mrs. S at the Housing Authority about getting her rent lowered to the amount it used to be and that a neighbor of hers had gotten her rent lowered. I asked Mrs. G if she understood how her public aid grant was budgeted. She said that all she knew was that she received $7 less each month, and that when you do not have much money, $7 is a lot to take away. I said that I hoped that I could help extend her grant.

I asked Mrs. G how she was feeling. She said that she was okay but that she was still having a lot of back pain. She said that the doctor gave her vitamins and that she had "low blood"; however, the doctor had not given her anything to make her feel less tired. I asked her if she had considered returning to her doctor and telling him that she does not have much energy. (I did not realize it then, but I had opened Pandora's box!)

She shook her head and said that she did not have the nerve to go to doctors, that she was scared of them. I asked her what she meant. She said that she did not know, that she just "hated going to them." I reminded her that she had gone to a doctor before and asked her if she was afraid then. She laughed and said she "sure was," but that she was "hurting so bad" she had to go. She kept talking about how frightened she was of doctors and how much she hated to go. I told her that many people were afraid of going to the doctor and that everyone who is afraid of doctors has some reason. I asked her what exactly she was afraid of. She said that she did not know why they poked and pinched. She does not like to undress in front of others and is afraid of what they might tell her. I asked her what she meant by "afraid of what they might tell her." She said that if something was "wrong with her" she would rather not know it. I asked her if she suspected that something was wrong with her. She told me that when the doctor examined her for the back problems, he also found a lump in her breast. When I asked when this occurred, she said seven or eight months ago and that she wasn't about to let anyone cut into her. She'd rather die. I asked her if the doctor explained to her what she should do about this lump. She said that she knew that it should be removed, but she wasn't even going to think about that. I asked her why not. She said that she was scared of surgery and that she thought they might find cancer. If she had cancer she would rather not know about it. Her understanding of cancer, I discovered, was "something that slowly eats your body away."

At this point, I felt that maybe I could help her understand what the removal of a breast tumor was all about. She had made some reference to wanting not to know what went on during surgery, and I asked her what she meant. Apparently, during the delivery of K, she was given a spinal, was semiconscious during the delivery, and did not like knowing what was happening. It scared her. I explained in simple language the surgical procedure to her, how a biopsy is taken, and told her that women often have tumors that are not cancerous and that surgery is a precautionary measure. I asked her what she thought was the very worst thing that could happen if indeed the lump were cancerous. She hung her head, looked embarrassed, and did not say anything. I was uncomfortable with the silence and finally told her that removal of a breast was, in some cases, necessary. She looked at me and said rather sarcastically that that didn't sound like a hell of a lot of fun. I assured her that I was in no way implying that it was a fun thing to go through and that being a woman I could understand her feelings. But I also pointed out that such difficulties could be dealt with and that she would still have a life to live.

I decided that this was all pretty serious business to be discussing on a first visit and felt that it was time to cool off a little. I asked her how she felt talking about this with me. She said okay, that she had not talked about it with anyone before, and that she was a little surprised that she was doing so now. I asked her whether she thought that her talking about it with me was perhaps an indication of how worried she actually was about the situation. She did not respond. I ended the conversation by saying that I was glad that we had shared this. I told her that I was in no way going to "order" her to go see a doctor. I asked her whether she thought maybe the two of us could talk about this again and perhaps work on her fear. She seemed to agree with this suggestion.

Mrs. G offered me a glass of water, as our throats were "dry" at this point. I asked her if her brother was still living with her. She said that he was and that the situation was working out okay. She indicated that he would be receiving unemployment compensation benefits in a few days and planned to contribute a small amount toward the rent and food. I inquired about his injury of some months ago. She said that he was doing okay but that his arm still bothered him. I suggested that perhaps during the next visit the three of us could get together. She said that that was okay with her and thought it would be okay with her brother.

Having been there for forty-five minutes, I decided that it was time to leave. I asked her how she felt about my visit and told her that the purpose of weekly visits would be to work through any difficulties that might be occurring. She said that her only real problem was lack of money. I suggested that maybe we meet every two weeks and see how that worked out. If she wanted to alter the meeting arrangement, she could. She still seemed hesitant, and I really felt that I was pushing. However, we set up an appointment for two weeks later. I told her that maybe we could think some more about doctor's visits. She then said that maybe she would surprise the two of us by going before the next visit. I told her that I did not want to leave the impression that she had to go to the doctor to please me. Ultimately, she might want to go for herself. We spent a few minutes discussing this. I then got up to go, telling her again that I was sorry for the mix-up with the time and thanking her for spending the time with me.

Assessment and Worker's Role

Mrs. G was cooperative and responsive, considering the delicate, personal matters that we discussed. Other than some financial help, she did not seem to know how I could help her. I must say that I really did not know either. While setting up a future appointment, I was very aware that this woman really believed that everything was going okay with her. I felt that I was in an awkward position and had the peculiar feeling that everything was not "okay" with her. However, if she thought everything was fine, who was I to tell her otherwise? Upon reflection, I realized that when she told me at the end of our interview that she did not have any problems except that of money, I should have said that what we were discussing sounded like a problem to me and then followed up. Perhaps then we could have made some sense out of why I was calling upon her in her home. I will keep these issues in mind when I make my next visit.

Plans

As soon as possible, I would like to see Mrs. G come to grips with the importance of her seeing a doctor about the lump on her breast. The lump is obviously on her mind; otherwise she would not have talked about it with me. She knows that we will discuss it again. After health problems are dealt with, she appears to be a good candidate for employment. She said during our visit that she had applied for a couple of factory jobs but that she did not know if she could work because she did not feel good. So her health comes first. If Mrs. G's brother is present during the next visit, I would like to know how he is and how long he will be receiving benefits. However, if he is present, the conversation between Mrs. G and myself concerning her fear of doctors and surgery may be postponed. I feel that I need a clearer picture of what their relationship is and whether or not he may need some help. Long-range plans include day-care services for K when Mrs. G is medically able to seek employment.

TEACHING FROM THE RECORDING

Purpose and Observation

The student states the purpose clearly and seems to understand the several concrete directions that she may take. However, later in the recording she indicates lack of clarity, despite having attempted to achieve the purpose stated.

The student's observation reflected a good description of the client and the physical surroundings. She clearly indicated her anxiety about the confusion with the appointment time, which can be explored further during a conference. The student should think about the effect of this on the client and alternative approaches. The possible significance of the client and her three-year-old child sleeping until 11:00 A.M. might also be discussed in the field-instruction conference.

Content

The student began by explaining her role to the client, which seemed stilted and no doubt rehearsed prior to arrival. Such behavior is expected from a beginning student on a first interview. The introduction of home visits on a weekly basis might frighten or threaten any client who did not clearly understand the service being offered, especially if the student is not certain of her role as an agency representative. The client did, however, identify her problem as financial, and she was able to state her confusion about her public aid grant. The student responded only by recognizing the difficulty (a positive), but she did not really address the issue presented by the client. This aspect of the visit should be discussed with the student; focus should be on how to handle questions and concerns raised by the client when the worker does not know the answers. A supportive stance on the part of the field instructor would help the student feel less threatened by not knowing and understand the process involved in learning the policies and procedures of other agencies.

Instead of dealing with the issues, the student moved into the feeling area in which she seemed to feel more comfortable. She involved the client appropriately in a dialogue about returning to the doctor for a follow-up visit on the back pain, which seemed intense. It appeared as though the client were waiting for the opportunity to unload her fears about the lump in her breast. The student picked up on the client's fear of doctors and uncovered the meaning through the use of clarification. Her intuitive capacity was evident in her demonstration of interest and concern. Clearly, the student's focus was on the client, and they communicated. Communication was hindered when the student proceeded with a somewhat detailed explanation of the medical procedure involved with breast tumors. The positives that should be identified in the field instruction conference include the student's sensitivity to the client's concern and her identification of this concern with the client. Speculating with the student about possible causes for the client's fears and ways in which these fears might be explored would stimulate the student to expand her perspective and enable her to see that others may not have the same orientation, viewpoint, and needs as she does. At this point, the stimulation should be directed toward helping the student think about her approach vs. other possibilities, rather than on taking the wrong approach or the need for changes in ways of doing.

The student demonstrates that she is somewhat aware that she is over her head and possibly out of her role when relaying lengthy medical information to the client. She was able to refocus the interview on the client's perceptions of the problem and the need to establish this problem as a future agenda item: "I decided that this was pretty serious business to be discussing on a first visit and felt it was time to cool off a little. I asked her how she felt talking about this with me." An excellent opportunity exists here for talking about the various roles of the social worker and the need for caution lest the worker overstep her boundaries. The potential role of advocate for the client in the health-care system should be highlighted.

The student seemed aware of the elements of the ending phases of an interview. This aspect of the visit can be tied in with classroom learning. Here again, the focus was more on the student than on what the client thought or wanted; however, the student did focus on areas for discussion during their next meeting. The student may need help in determining what issues are appropriate to discuss.

Assessment and Worker's Role

The student is open and honest in her evaluation and should be commended for this. The field instructor can verify what was picked up throughout the content section; that is, the student has good intuitive skills but needs help in bringing these skills to a conscious level. For example, she was aware of something not being right with the client but unsure of what to do with this "gut" feeling. Although the student stated her purpose clearly, she was, in fact, not at all sure about her reasons for being there. The student's realization that she did not clearly understand her role, as well as other ideas that she presented, indicate good potential for learning and some awareness of her need to make changes. The student is able to establish goals and set priorities. The field instructor can help by discussing timing and readiness of the client to take action, that is, "as soon as possible" may take months. Conference time should be spent on clarifying the agency's policies and procedures as well as those of the income-maintenance programs in the community.

In summary, the interview can help the field instructor individualize the learner and begin to assess the student's learning patterns and evaluate the student's level of maturity, knowledge, understanding, and skill. The field instructor's assumption that this student is sensitive; capable of recall; supportive; and free to share her perceptions, anxiety, and thinking is important. Although her knowledge of agency policy and community resources is not very evident, the student was able to elicit feeling and quickly touch on a sensitive area with the client. Both parties were aware of the interaction process. The student appeared free to risk. She may not be very aware of her intuitive skills; she needs help learning how to move at the client's pace, to use direct influence more appropriately, and to bring theory into better balance with feeling content.

STUDENT LEARNING FROM RECORDING

The student admitted that her initial reaction to the interview was one of disappointment. This disappointment was based primarily on the intensity of her feelings about the client's medical problem and the fact that the client expressed ambivalence about setting up another appointment. Her fantasy was that the client would express appreciation for the worker's interest and concern, would realize the immediacy of her problem, and would indicate her need for ongoing contact.

During the process of writing the recording, the student began to realize that she did not truly understand her role. She felt no particular identification with the agency and felt uncomfortable because she could not immediately meet the client's concrete requests (increase in rent and clothing assistance). The student knew, however, that the client had numerous problems but was unsure about her role in helping the client deal with these problems. However, the student had no doubt about the need to return for follow-up contacts, despite the client's hesitancy.

The discussion of the recording was helpful to the student in a number of ways. She was relieved that the field instructor had picked up on her feelings of discouragement and floundering in her role. As the positives of the interview were identified — the student's openness in the recording, sensitivity to the medical problem, ability to maintain focus, and so forth — the student was able to relax and respond to feedback on areas that might have been handled differently. Also, a connection could be made between the student's not knowing how other agencies operate and discomfort in her role. The student was able to discuss her fears about breast cancer and understand that some of these fears were projected onto the client. This was a revelation that permitted her to see where her role stopped and the medical professional took over. This aspect of the visit was an excellent opening for discussion of social work principles and the various roles of the social worker.

The student was pleased as well as amazed that so much emphasis was placed on her strengths. She had not thought in terms of her strengths and admitted to feeling some apprehension that the field instructor would not approve of her interview. However, she was not sure what had gone wrong. This confusion presented an opportunity to reclarify the role of the field instructor, which consequently was more meaningful to the student.

In conclusion, the process recording helped the student begin to understand her strengths, reinforce her self-confidence, and give direction to areas that needed to be observed and worked on. The student realized that her expectations for both client and self were too high, and she achieved some awareness that changes involve both time and process. In addition, the student admitted to learning through the recording.

APPENDIX B
SAMPLE RECORDING TO PREPARE FOR PROFESSIONAL PRACTICE

Case name: Mrs. K
Dates: 2/5, 2/12

Areas covered in interview (related to purpose? explain)	Client's concerns identified; how handled by worker	Conclusions or resolutions to concerns; plan
Sick baby	Mrs. K is concerned that the baby is frequently ill. The baby had to be hospitalized again; the doctor thinks it might be allergies. We talked about what hospitalization means to Mrs. K. At first she viewed problems as only physical in nature, but in interview 2 she admitted that she needed to learn how to physically care for the baby. She likes to play with the	Mrs. K. agreed to explore with the worker some different approaches to caring for the baby: schedule, food, bathing, and communicating with the doctor. May need to consider homemaker–teacher but wants to try the above first. Further exploration of her fear that the baby will be taken from her is necessary. (Does she fear baby will die?)

Areas covered in interview (related to purpose? explain)	Client's concerns identified; how handled by worker	Conclusions or resolutions to concerns; plan
	baby but the responsibility is difficult for her. She is afraid the baby may be taken from her and does not know how to question the doctor.	
Housing and management	Mrs. K wants own apartment. She is unrealistic in approach and considerations, and she is determined to separate from her mother. She wants five rooms and own furniture. Both interviews focused on evaluating pros and cons of remaining in the neighborhood or moving a distance from the mother and on apartment size and rental in terms of her small grant. Worker went with her to check out several apartments, with emphasis on how to question landlord and what to look for.	Mrs. K. decided that she wanted the unfurnished apartment in the building with mother. She is still unrealistic and unable to see the consequences of such a plan from a financial point of view. (Adolescent striving for independence.) Important to continue to deal with lack of reality, especially when she tries to manage on the few dollars left in her grant for food and other expenses.

Sample Recording to Prepare for Professional Practice

Areas covered in interview (related to purpose? explain)	Client's concerns identified; how handled by worker	Conclusions or resolutions to concerns; plan
Relationship with mother and deceased sister. (The first two areas that were covered were related to purpose. The area dealing with relationship evolved from the discussions of housing in interview 2.)	Mrs. K's ambivalent feelings about her mother; feelings of loss for her sister (two years older than Mrs. K) who died of leukemia. Mrs. K. expressed a lot of anger toward her mother, who left her to be raised by a grandmother until she was twelve years old, when the mother remarried. Worker let her talk and attempted to clarify how client viewed her mother's role (more like sibling). Her expressed feelings around death of sister were the first instance of real sharing. She cried and said she felt deserted by the sister. Worker gave lots of recognition to Mrs. K's being able to talk about this but did not feel able to follow up on this loss.	We identified Mrs. K's grief as an area to be further discussed. The plan is to help Mrs. K gain some objectivity in her relationship with the mother and deal with her loss. (Not sure how to approach these issues. There has been so much loss in her life.)

APPENDIX C
ROLE PLAY

Client: Mr. B (Field Instructor)

Social Worker: Undergraduate Student

Setting: Private Child Welfare Agency

Identifying Information: Mr. B, a married father of three children, came to the office on 10/2. He said that he wanted to become involved in the foster care program. He seemed to be seeking information about the program.

PROCESS RECORDING

Purpose

To determine whether Mr. B would be sufficiently capable of caring for a foster child (financially, emotionally, and so forth). To determine whether he meets the licensing requirements.

Observation

Mr. B presented himself as a very capable individual who would be able to handle the responsibilities of a foster child. Mr. B was very comfortable throughout the interview. I also got the impression that he was "in charge" at home. When I asked whether foster care was a joint decision between him and his wife, he responded that he was the one who made the decisions in the home, and his wife would go along with anything he decided. Mr. B also impressed me as being well educated and articulate. He stated that he had a master's degree and that his wife also had completed four years of college.

Content

I began by introducing myself and explaining the function of the Home Finding Unit. Also, I explained that the purpose of the interview was to determine whether Mr. B met the requirements for being a foster parent. To begin with, I inquired about his family. He is married and has three daughters. His oldest daughter is seven years old and the younger two are of preschool age. Mr. B stated that the reason he was interested in foster care was that he wanted a boy. At this point, I probably should have asked if he was planning to have any more children of his own. More important, I should have explained that foster care is really "temporary care." Did he realize that if he did take a boy into his home that every effort would be made to move the child back to his natural home as quickly as possible?

After we discussed his family, I directed the conversation to how much space he had available for another child. He said that he had bought a house last June and that it had five bedrooms. He explained that he and his wife share a bedroom and the three girls share another room. Therefore, he would have at least three bedrooms available. I probably should have asked about how the house was being financed. The mortgage payments might have placed a financial strain on the family.

Next, I explained that a family must be able to financially support a child. Although I explained that foster parents receive a payment for board, I also pointed out that this money does not cover all of the expenses. Mr. B did not seem to understand why the agency or the state did not pay all the bills. He seemed to be quite upset by this fact. I tried to explain that spending the family's own money indicated that the family was really committed to the child. I really was not sure how to handle his hostility; however, I was pleased that I did not take the attack personally.

After discussing the issue of financial stability, I brought up the time appropriateness of entering the foster care program. At this point, I asked about any recent death, miscarriage, or change in employment. Mr. B appeared to comply with these requirements.

Next, I asked about Mr. B's family. He stated that he was from the East Coast. He has one brother who still lives in the East. Aside from periodic visits, he rarely has any contact with his family. I also thought it was interesting to note that the first thing Mr. B mentioned was that he came from a two-parent home. This might be an indication that he did come from a stable environment. However, I would need a lot more information before I could make this assumption.

Mr. B also talked about his wife's background. Her family originates from California and she has limited contact with her family. I wondered about what effect this lack of family ties had on the Bs. In a home study, I need to find out how Mr. and Mrs. B were raised. I would also like to know why they both moved to Chicago away from their families. In addition, I need more specific information about relatives (names, birth dates, and so forth).

One important area that I really did not obtain much information about is the B's marital relationship. In the home study, I need to look at the interactions among family members. Also, I would like to know how the power is distributed. Mr. B gave me the impression that he was in charge at home. How does he relate to his wife and the children? What is prompting the family to explore the agency's foster care program?

Finally, I explained the process of becoming foster parents. Mr. B seemed adamantly against the idea of both he and his wife coming to the foster parent orientation meeting. The reason for this resistance was partly my fault. At first, I explained that he and his wife would be "invited" to this meeting. When he said he was too busy to come, I made it clear that rather than just an invitation, this meeting was a requirement. I also thought that I was not too clear about the purpose of the meeting; therefore I did not seem very convincing about why this meeting was important.

At this time, I began to explain the foster care system in general terms. Before the interview, I was not sure whether this explanation should take place before or after I discussed the requirements. I was not as clear as I at first thought I was about the steps of the foster care program. This lack of clarity was evident when Mr. B asked me questions about the program. Fortunately, this time the "client" was able to explain the system to me.

I ended the interview by summing up what we had talked about. I also interjected that I thought Mr. B was a potential foster parent.

Assessment and Worker's Role

Mr. B seemed to be a possible candidate for the role of foster parent. However, a complete home study must be done in order to determine whether Mr. and Mrs. B are in compliance with the licensing standards. Two areas of particular concern are the reasons for Mr. B wanting only boys and whether Mrs. B wants to participate in the foster care program. Does she even want any more children?

I felt quite disorganized. I was afraid that I was jumping from one topic to another much too quickly. Also, I need to find out when I should explain the foster care program to the client. Finally,

I need to slow down and pay more attention to the specifics, such as names, ages, dates, and the like. On the other hand, I felt that I handled Mr. B's hostility rather well. I was able to bring out many of the requirements that foster parents must meet.

Plans
I plan to send Mr. and Mrs. B a letter with three possible dates to choose from for a foster parent orientation meeting.

STUDENT'S RESPONSE TO THE ROLE PLAY

The role play with my field instructor was certainly a valuable learning experience. First of all, it helped me learn the licensing requirments for foster care much more quickly. Second, it showed that I needed to organize the information obtained according to the home-study outline. The practice interview also gave me the opportunity to try out different questions so that I might determine if they elicited the needed information, as well as the opportunity to field appropriate questions. My field instructor asked questions that many prospective foster parents might ask, which tested my command of the material and allowed me to see the areas in which I was weak. For example, I thought that I knew what the purpose of the foster parent orientation meeting was; however, when it came down to explaining the meeting, I realized that I was unclear about the specifics.

The practice interview gave me the opportunity to compare my own style of interviewing with another worker's style of interviewing. The feedback from my field instructor helped me realize how my questions made him feel and made me aware of the effect of my feelings on the interview.

FIELD INSTRUCTOR'S RESPONSE TO THE ROLE PLAY

This type of role play was definitely a valuable learning tool both for the student and for me. It gave the student much needed practice in interviewing. Since it took place within the agency, it allowed the student to make mistakes and learn from them. I was able to see how much the student had learned about agency procedures and requirements as well as evaluate the effectiveness of the student's interviewing skills and the areas in which the student needed to improve.

Role playing was an excellent way for me to observe the student's capacity to risk, assess, and speculate. Through the process recording and the conference that followed, I was able to demonstrate the role of field instruction and how the learning/teaching process would proceed throughout the academic year. The role-play activity allowed us to participate together. The student was free to consider the importance of facts and feelings and to draw on some of the theory covered in class and readings. The student was able to talk about messages in the role play that were difficult to pick up on and handle, and we were able to determine together that this area needs further attention.

This student is ready to take responsibility for her own learning. I felt eager to teach someone whom I anticipated would be invested and involved in the learning.

I. FUNCTIONING WITH THE AGENCY

	More than adequate	Adequate	Less than adequate
Understanding of the structure and function of the agency:	____	____	____

- appreciation of agency's historical development in relation to current practices
- understanding of the organizational dynamics within the agency and the processes involved in change
- understanding of the basic policies and procedures of the agency and professional services to other social agencies and community

Ability to evaluate strengths and limitations of the agency's program and services in achieving its goals and in meeting the needs of clients:	____	____	____

- commitment to maintaining the professional standards of the agency and to questioning the appropriate agency personnel when standards appear to be discordant with the values and ethics of the profession

Ability to assume responsibilities for management of work load and relationships with colleagues:	____	____	____

- follows through on agency procedures as they relate to the client system relationships with intervention system, staff, and peers

Ability to assume responsibility for management of time:	____	____	____

- prompt at office
- keeps appointments with clients
- completes required agency forms and recording
- arranges coverage when not in office
- organizes assignments so that maximum services are provided to all clients

Respond, in a narrative paragraph, to the student's performance in the above areas. Provide specific examples of the strengths and limitations of the student's learning. Identify goals for continued development.

Level of competency: ____ More than adequate
____ Adequate
____ Less than adequate

B. Collection, Organization, and Analysis of Data:

Development of data collection techniques:

- questioning properly
- observational skills
- proper use of existing recorded material

Ability to organize data for assessment purposes

Ability to analyze the client-problem situation in relation to:

- background information
- effects of external elements on the problematic situation
- effects of cultural factors, racism, sexism, and other biases on the situation
- the degree to which formal and informal societal resources have provided services to the client system
- capacity and ability of the client system
- capacity and ability of the client to cope with the stress of the problem situation
- defensive operations of the client system
- maintaining a frame of reference based on professional ethics throughout the assessment process

C. Selection and Implementation of Intervention Plan:

Ability to use the problem assessment as a basis for a clear statement of objectives and for establishing an intervention plan for the client

Ability to identify an approach to intervention and to use it purposefully in attaining stated objectives

- flexible use of self in various roles to facilitate change
- involves other systems appropriately in the problem-solving process

Ability to help the client become increasingly involved in problem solving and decision making through continued use of processes such as the following:

- clarification of the target problem
- partialization of the problem into elements
- identification of problem-solving alternatives
- interpretation of resources and services that can be brought to bear on the target problems
- using advice giving, instruction, information, and supportive techniques appropriately

Ability to use the interview or group situation to facilitate progress toward attainment of stated objectives:

- clarity of purpose
- focus
- appropriate questioning
- sensitivity to communication patterns
- engagement of all members in the communication process
- provides for concrete needs
- identifies and deals with feeling areas
- plans the next session

Ability to deal with case termination, including the worker's handling of his or her response to separation   _____   _____   _____

D. Evaluation of Interventive Efforts, Feedback:

Recognition of the need to evaluate results of interventive efforts: _____   _____   _____

- looks at own role in the helping process and the outcome of the intervention model selected
- involves the client system in evaluating the results of help
- assesses agency services in relation to the needs of clients
- evaluates the existing community resource system in relation to the needs of clients

Willingness to look at social issues and welfare policy and his or her role in this area   _____   _____   _____

Respond, in a narrative paragraph, to the student's performance in the above areas. Provide specific examples of the strengths and limitations of the student's learning. Identify goals for continued development.

Level of competency: _____ More than adequate
                                  _____ Adequate
                                  _____ Less than adequate

Undergraduate Field-Practice Evaluation Form 177

IV. LEARNING

	More than adequate	Adequate	Less than adequate

Learning through field instruction: _____   _____   _____

- assumes responsibility for learning, that is, shares ideas and concerns in conference, follows through on suggestions from the field instructor, and takes initiative in decision making and planning
- tolerates objective evaluations made by those who facilitate the learning experience
- evaluates self in overall learning and performance, including strengths and limitations

Learning through field experience: _____   _____   _____

- transfers learning from one situation to another
- quality of recording for learning/teaching purposes
- quality of letter writing and summary recordings for agency purposes
- evaluates learning from field experience, that is, identifies and relates to problems in working through obstacles to learning and appreciates the importance of continued learning for development of knowledge and skills

Learning through professional and peer groups: _____   _____   _____

- ability to help constructively in presenting ideas and opinions
- comfortable sharing ideas with others and respectful of the